Overcoming Betrayal

The Breakthrough Therapeutic Approach

A Couples' Guide to Healing from Both Perspectives

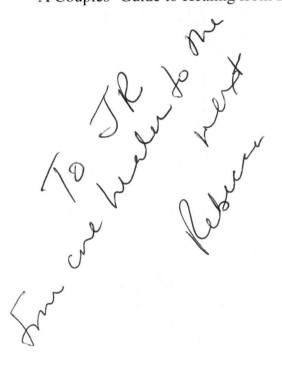

Rebecca Rosenblat

Psychotherapist, Infidelity & Sex Addiction Counselor, TV Host

Foreword by Dr. Douglas Weiss

Library and Archives Canada Cataloguing in Publication

Rosenblat, Rebecca, author
  Overcoming betrayal : the breakthrough
therapeutic approach / Rebecca
Rosenblat.

Includes bibliographical references.
ISBN 978-1-988058-25-2 (hardcover).

--ISBN 978-1-988058-26-9 (softcover)

  1. Couples therapy. 2. Betrayal--Psychological
aspects. I. Title.

 RC488.5.R65 2017
616.89'1562   C2017-902138-9

Printed and bound in Canada / First Edition.
Cover Design-layout-Interior-edit: Michael Davie
240 pages. Approximately 51,000 words. All rights reserved.
Published April 5, 2017
Manor House Publishing Inc.
452 Cottingham Crescent, Ancaster, ON, L9G 3V6
www.manor-house.biz
(905) 648-2193

"This project has been made possible [in part] by the Government of Canada. «
Ce projet a été rendu possible [en partie] grâce au gouvernement du Canada."

Funded by the Government of Canada
Financé par le gouvernement du Canada |

Dedicated to all those who have the courage to hang in and build something better than ever before!
- Rebecca Rosenblat

Acknowledgements

Thanks to all those who opened up their hearts to me, and trusted me enough to allow me into the most intimate parts of their lives, so we could heal wounds and build resiliency together. It was such an honour and a privilege to work with you, and watch you go places you never thought possible! Thanks also to my mentors and colleagues who lent me their ears, when the pain all around me became unbearable.

And last, but definitely not least, thanks to my publisher, Michael Davie, for believing in me and being patient with my umpteen changes; and my family for always being supportive, especially when I had to hibernate to write.

God bless you all!

ENDORSEMENTS

"I appreciated Rebecca's openness to discuss infidelity from both perspectives. I believe she's the first to walk through the process holding both realities together, while doing an amazing job informing couples of issues to address, as well as giving them a roadmap to address these issues. Anyone who has experienced infidelity would do well to read Overcoming Betrayal."

~ **Dr. Douglas Weiss**, President of the American Association for Sex Addiction Therapy (AASAT)

"With Overcoming Betrayal Rebecca provides a soup-to-nuts look at infidelity in a committed relationship, bringing years of experience and examining both sides of the issue – his and hers alike – with intelligence and compassion. By the end, she provides not only understanding but a recipe for healing and rebuilding relationship trust."

~ **Robert Weiss**, Author of *Sex Addiction 101* and *Out of the Doghouse: A Step-by-Step Relationship-Saving Guide for Men Caught Cheating*

"Rebecca captures the true essence of infidelity from both sides. She unfolds the personal stories of pain, sadness, grief and ultimately healing and rebuilding. This book is a gift to all couples who are working through infidelity."

~ **Debbie Allen,** Certified Sex Addiction Therapist

"Overcoming Betrayal is a one of a kind book, that no one else dared to write. The book opened up my world to becoming a much better person, and my relationship much healthier. My partner has finally found a book she can understand and which answers her questions. All my blessing to Rebecca."

~ **WS,** In recovery

"A dialectic is the ability to hold two seemingly opposite thoughts together at the same time." This is an academic endeavour. Rarely does it involve empathy, or even ask for empathy, which is what makes this book such a true gem. Rebecca has so eloquently and with such grace and respect, been able to bring what is too often in the counselling room, a war of two worlds and offer a bridge of meaningful peace and hope. An intelligent read for therapists and a must read for couples who find themselves in this situation."

~ **Mark Laing**, Registered Psychotherapist, Couples and Sex Addictions

Table of Contents

Foreword

When someone experiences infidelity, whether it's due to an affair or as a result of sexual addiction, there is a significant amount of pain and many questions that come up.

Through those times in your life, you want to have a friend. Not just *any* friend, but one who knows you and knows the pain you're going through.

Just the presence of this wise friend is soothing to the soul. That's what Rebecca provides through her book, *Overcoming Betrayal*.

Rebecca has brought together her years of experience and knowledge, in a heartfelt, intelligent manner, to help those who've experienced infidelity.

Rebecca shares a couple's journey, who've experienced the betrayal of infidelity. She introduces you to this couple – John and Jane – through her first session with them.

Then, and this is really the most helpful part of this book, Rebecca takes the reader by the hand and lets you walk with this couple through the recovery and healing process.

Rebecca presents, in the fairest way that I have read to date, his side of the issues as well as hers.

Rebecca takes this balanced approach without shame or blame, in a genuinely caring and honest way, where each person can see where they are and grow.

I appreciated Rebecca's openness to discuss infidelity from both perspectives of an affair and as a result of an addiction.

As well, I believe Rebecca is the *first* to walk through this process holding both realities together for couples that have experienced infidelity.

Overall, this book has done an amazing job informing couples of issues to address, as well as giving them a roadmap to address these issues.

Anyone who has experienced infidelity would do well to read *Overcoming Betrayal*.

- **Douglas Weiss**, Ph.D., President of the American Association for Sex Addiction Therapy (AASAT)

Book Summary

When a betrayal rocks a relationship – be it due to an affair or sex addiction – the couple needs to work together to get through it. But feeling hurt, upset, and afraid dissuades both parties from being exposed and vulnerable to each other – the very ingredients that are critical to healing. And most books are generally directed at the partner's pain and healing, the wounding party's recovery, or a clinical view of the couple-ship.

This book is intended to bring both parties together, by understanding each other's mindset, feeling each other's pain, and finding the answers that couples look for when their world has been blown apart.

Using a powerful combination of both theory and story, you'll be able to connect with the emotions of our composite couple (based on hundreds of couples that Rebecca has seen), understand the emotions that betrayals stir up, and ultimately learn how to navigate through them, to come together to a place of healing, that's better than anything you thought possible.

The book starts off with a bit more theory to give you guidance, and ends with the perfect story, that'll give you both hope and healing.

It's a must read for any couple who wants to find their way back to each other! There isn't another book quite like it, that'll take you to the heart of your emotions, answer your questions, and help you heal in a life-transforming way. It's the ultimate couple bible to take you from a place of darkness to a place of light, that's full of the joy and happiness you never thought possible.

Yes, you can get there, and you can learn to trust again!

"The wounds of the injured become the wounds of the relationship, inflicting pain on both parties. If only the betrayed could see what goes on in the mind of the betrayer, and vice versa, they could heal each other. But neither party feels safe enough to risk that level of vulnerability!"

- Rebecca Rosenblat

Introduction

Passion, intensity, excitement, sexual tension – the ingredients that shows like *Scandal* and *The Affair* use to make betrayal feel oh-so-seductive!

In reality, betrayal is anything but seductive; take it from me, a psychotherapist who specializes in dealing with the aftermath, day in and day out – the ache that won't go away, the doubts that forever haunt you, the berating and condemnation, which replace love and admiration.

The wounds of the injured become the wounds of the relationship, inflicting pain on *both* parties. If only the betrayed could see what goes on in the mind of the betrayer, and vice versa, they could heal each other. But neither party feels safe enough to risk *that* level of vulnerability!

This book is intended to go where no man or woman has gone before, right into the heart of that unexplored territory; to unmask those vulnerabilities from *both* sides, answer difficult questions, and build trust and healing, when it feels nearly impossible!

Meet John and Jane, composite characters, which embody hundreds of real couples that I've worked with, who share virtually identical themes and journeys.

Hopefully, they'll offer deep insights into the minds of both parties, on either side of betrayal, allowing you to gain an understanding into each other – the why's, the hurt, the recovery – and forge a relationship that's better than anything you had before; beyond what you ever thought possible!

Couples often tell me that as twisted as it sounds, the devastation from the betrayal was the best thing that ever happened to them – it was a wakeup call that allowed them to focus on what they cherish the most, and do whatever they needed to fix it; ultimately reaching that magical place that lived beyond their wildest dreams! And *that's* always my hope and goal for them (as it is for you), even as they say, "We wanna go back to the way we were in the beginning" – not what I'd pick, because it's that very non-authentic course that took them to a place they never intended.

But before we begin, I want to highlight three key points. Firstly, although our main characters are John and Jane, their journey isn't intended to be sexist or heteronormative, because both sides come from both genders, and many parts of them come from LGBTQ couples. Secondly, we'll be moving back and forth between affairs and sex addiction, because while the sting of betrayal may feel similar, the "whys" are anything but; necessitating different explanations and recovery work – therapists who treat them as the same can do more harm than good. Finally, since I'm trained as a Certified Sex Addiction Therapist through IITAP – International Institute of Trauma and Addiction Professionals – I'll be referencing their highly successful treatment protocol from time to time.

Let's begin our journey now.

Happy trails!

- Rebecca Rosenblat

Chapter 1

The First Visit to the Therapist's Office

We've all heard the saying that every coin has two sides – no one knows that better than someone who works with couples struck by betrayal.

The irony: those individuals often don't know how true that statement really is; and may not have a clue around what their partner's feeling, even with respect to themselves.

We seem to think that we know ourselves better than anyone else. While that may be true of our conscious brain, the nuances that our subconscious brain puts out – the stuff we can't control – is possibly better known to our partner, even when they choose to wear blinders.

I can't tell you how many times I've heard someone say, "I knew something was off – I could feel it in my gut – but my partner told me I was imagining things."

And since almost everything's on the table by the time they come to see me, the betrayer almost always responds with, "It's like he/she had a radar of sorts, that picked up on subtle stuff every single time; but I always made sure I nipped everything in the bud, making her/him believe that they were just imagining things."

The official term for making one's partner feel like they're crazy, when they're picking up on something that's actually there, is, "gaslighting" – based on a 1944 film, *Gaslight*, starring Ingrid Bergman.

Bergman's on-screen husband wants to get his hands on her jewelry, and realizes that the only way to accomplish that is by having her certified as insane, and hauled off to a mental institution. So he intentionally sets the gaslights in their home to flicker on and off – and every time Bergman's character reacts to it, he tells her she's just seeing things.

While in that situation, the gaslighter was presenting false information, the term is generally used to refer to *any* intentional attempts to make someone doubt themselves.

For instance, by telling them that they're too sensitive, emotional, dramatic, irrational, over-reacting, freaking out for no reason, acting stupid, imagining things, etc. etc. – remarks which are used to shut one down, via emotional manipulation. It can leave them feeling insecure and/or irrational.

And since nobody wants to feel that way about themselves, they'd rather not say anything at all, so they end up dismissing themselves and their feelings as unimportant; both of which impact relationships in profound ways.

Gaslighting behaviors almost always come up in the very first session, since going against our gut feelings feels like a betrayal against ourselves, which is a lot harder to stomach – if we can't trust ourselves, who can we trust? Certainly not the party who's hurt us; and been untrustworthy! It mars many a partner's ability to trust their own judgement.

John and Jane were no different; she felt almost more enraged about that, than the story we were about to get into.

John's and Jane's First Visit with Me

I always start off my first session with, "What brings you here today?". At that point, more often than not, both parties look at each other in a puzzled way – as if they haven't a clue. ... After several awkward seconds, the injured party invariably says to the betrayer, "Do *you* want to tell her, since it's because of what *you* did?"

At that point, shame takes over and renders the betrayer nearly speechless, and the partner takes over. ... From there on, it's a crap shoot – either the betrayer continues to let them vent, or takes over, because he/she can't tolerate to witness the palpable pain. Either way, I get the punch line before I get the details.

In John's and Jane's case, he said, "I cheated on her!".

Jane broke down crying. She was barely coherent, as she tried to speak through her sobs. I offered her a Kleenex and just quietly listened.

I know it's a really tough and courageous act to open up to a stranger. So I just allow people to get things off their chest, without interrupting, since they've likely rehearsed the speech before – even though they may look dumbfounded – to ensure that they get everything out at get go. Occasionally, it starts out with "I don't know where to begin", and then, with a little bit of encouragement from me, it ends up in the same place.

Jane shared that she first wrote off John's irritability to stress at work, his disengagement to being distracted by the same, and his lack of sexual interest to him being exhausted. His late nights at the computer, and him having a more intense relationship with his smart phone than with her, only confirmed a possible work crisis. All she had to do was wait it out and the situation would pass. But that never happened.

John spent more and more time on his electronic devices, was later and later coming home; and when he did, he was distant. Eventually, Jane asked John if something was wrong, expecting him to share that his job was on the line. But he became very upset with her, accusing her of adding her *imaginary* worries to his *real* problems, creating an issue where there was none, taking away from the important things he needed to concentrate on.

At that point, Jane moved back and forth between feeling that something was off and feeling that she was simply crazy. Either way, it didn't feel good for her, but she was too scared to rock the boat. So she tried instead to take things into her own hands to regain his interest, so he'd find his way back to her, from whatever was distracting him so much. Jane started to work out more, planned romantic evenings, and started sexting John with promises of things to come.

John was pleased with Jane's efforts, and they managed to have some of the best, knock-your-socks-off sex they'd ever had; with more urgency than what they'd experienced even through the initial groping stages in their late teens, when Mother Nature was dousing them with feel-good-hormones, to con them into mating. Naturally, Jane assumed things were back on track, since *she'd* inspired John after all.

As the days went by, something still felt a bit off; even as John started to initiate sex more and more often, albeit in the form of disengaged quickies, since "that's all he had the time and energy for."

But then, that too became less frequent, leaving Jane baffled yet again, until the day she caught him masturbating in front of his computer. Shocked and horrified, she questioned him why he chose to do that, when she was right there, yearning for him. John shared that it was *she* who he really wanted, but he was too tired to take care of her, so he decided to take care of himself "to take the edge off" instead of using her, or pissing her off by rushing through it yet again. Although that sounded plausible to Jane, since she *had* expressed her desire to have something "more meaningful" from time to time, it left her feeling a bit perturbed all the same, because John never even gave her a choice – just left her high and dry so to speak!

Eventually, Jane got tired of waiting for John – to chat about her day – and started enjoying chatting with her neighbour, Nick, who was paying her the kind of attention she craved from John, that wasn't forthcoming. With time, Nick wanted more. But out of respect for his wife, Jane wasn't willing to cross the skin-to-skin line with him, even though their emotional affair had crossed many other lines.

Meanwhile, John's indiscretions continued on. Initially they were just digital, so he felt "he wasn't cheating". Eventually, they became intensely physical, but he rationalized those by blaming Jane for not being there for him – at his beck and call, as she saw it - which only infuriated her.

According to Jane, John wanted her to be ever-present to him, even though he didn't have the aptitude to be present to her – but the disconnect was enough for him to resent her and build an entitlement to get attention elsewhere.

In the beginning, John became used to feeling really special to Jane; so when he stopped feeling that way and someone else seduced him with attention, it was an aphrodisiac that he simply couldn't resist. He became enslaved to it; soon, the ego stroking transitioned to libido stroking – and the rest as they say is history.

Once Jane got all that off her chest, I finally said, "Thanks for sharing – I appreciate how hard it must've been for you."

With the story out of the way, Jane moved onto sharing her feelings. "Hard doesn't' even cut it! ... I was completely blindsided by the double life he'd been living – finding out about it was devastating and traumatic. I couldn't breathe. My life was over, so I just wanted to kill myself and be done with it. How could he have done this to me – a wife who'd stood by him through the toughest times – just for a few moments of pleasure here and there? I catapulted from seeing him as my beloved – the center of my universe – to the source of my shock, anger, resentment, grief, and at times hatred for what I was going through. What's worse: when everything crashed in that cataclysmic moment of discovery, I couldn't turn to my best friend for support – the one person I thought I could always count on to protect me and have my back – since *he's* the one who made my world come crashing down, after repeatedly looking into my eyes and reassuring me that nothing was wrong, and that I was insane for thinking so."

Hearing Jane share like that had a huge impact on John – he started to cry, his head hung down in shame. Jane looked at him, but had a hard time reaching out to him. After I gave John a Kleenex, she looked up at me, to see if she could keep going.

I asked John if he needed a moment. He shook his head and said, "Please let her finish."

Jane continued with, "I felt raw, vulnerable, broken, empty, horrified, and hoped it was all a nightmare that I'd wake up from; but everything was real, right down to the last painful detail – completely out of my control and inescapable. The fear of the unknown terrified me; knowing that my entire marriage was a fraud enraged me. I repeatedly asked myself, 'What am I going to do?'"

Jane shuddered, and then went on to say, "The thought of him touching me disgusted me. I took off my wedding ring and allowed my mind to think about what it would feel like to be with someone else, instead of a shadow of a man who'd held my head under water for all these years; but he'd robbed me of that as well, because I couldn't trust anyone, and because he made me feel ugly, undesirable, inadequate, and ashamed – it was one of the worst things he'd done to me."

John looked up and barely mouthed, "I'm sorry."

Jane couldn't bear to look at John. She just needed to get all her feelings out. I totally got that – if you can't tell your therapist exactly how you're feeling, then what's the point, right?

Jane sighed, blew out her nose, and started sharing again. 'The bitter rage consumed me. John saw that and said, 'I'm willing to do anything to make this right, but I'm afraid that anything short of me blowing my brains out won't convince you of how sorry I am.' I finally saw his frustration and realized that I hadn't given him much to work with, to make things right. So here we are, hoping that you can show us what to do."

I put my hand on Jane's shoulder and said, "I'm really glad that you came. We'll get through this."

I looked over at John and asked if he was ready to share what *he* was feeling – and his side of the story.

John nodded, head still looking at the floor, and took a deep breath before staring. "I missed Jane. Once the kids came they filled her heart, hugged her soul, and cuddled away her need for connection. And then there was work, chores, social media, electronics – those damn electronics! Everything else seemed to matter more to her than me. Bottom line, I stopped feeling special to her – I guess, life also got in the way. So I decided to go online myself, to escape, even though I'd complained about it when *she* did it, knowing full well how insignificant it'd made me feel, when her fingers caressed her iPod in bed instead of caressing me ... or when she laughed at jokes others sent to her, instead of paying attention to my jokes.

"At first, it was just looking, then cyber chatting, then texting, then sexting, then chatting for real, and eventually .... It felt good to be desired for a change ... feel carefree, and escape the mundane demands of everyday life. But not once did I think that Jane was probably feeling the same emptiness – truth be told, I didn't think of Jane at all, and had convinced myself that she wasn't thinking of me either. So when stress got me down, I tried to escape in my own way – I thought I was doing her a favour by not bugging her ... almost like I deserved a medal for it. I suppose if I was to look deep down, I'd have to admit that part of me wanted to hurt her, for setting me aside, and making everything else more important than me."

John let out a sarcastic chuckle, "Do you see how the medal thing makes sense, since I was a martyr – a good guy who made good money, wasn't abusive to her in any way, helped with chores, and even babysat ... yes, I see the irony in that, since they were my kids too, and when she looked after them she wasn't "babysitting" them. ... But damn it, when a guy works hard all day, isn't he allowed to have some 'me time' to decompress, instead of being greeted at the door with a 'to do' list, or being yelled at for not keeping up – made to feel like a loser! ... And that right there led to me feeling entitled in some way. ... The sad thing of it is, when I finally realized what I'd done to her, I ended up feeling like the biggest loser on my own – she didn't have to convince me. It led to unbearable pain, and petrifying fear of losing her and the kids. I'd cry when no one was around, and even started to have panic attacks, but I couldn't share any of it with her; after all, *I* was the creator of my own misery. She'd be furious at the thought of me looking for sympathy.

"So I became stuck in the feeling that I'd done this bad thing, and as such had lost all my rights to speak up, even when she was wrong about me. I let her play whack-a-mole with me, even as I got tired of her reading my mind incorrectly, in the worst way imaginable – hell, I'd hate me (worse than I already did) if there was any truth to some of her accusations – but I wasn't exactly speaking up, since I was convinced that would cause a fight. So the vicious cycle continued, and with it, intense resentment and severe pain, on both sides, I'm sure. ... But then there were times when she seemed to check out – I guess all that emotional intensity was exhausting her – but I couldn't do the same; the searing pain was constant, making it impossible for me to escape, or forgive myself. ... I guess it's true what they say, 'Forgiveness is giving up the need for sufficient punishment' whatever that amount may be – damn if I know, because I haven't gotten there just yet. ... So what I'm hoping for is, that you'll help me heal Jane's pain, and show her that I'm done hurting her. ... Not sure what I was thinking before; all those exhausting lies, keeping secrets straight (with the right cover stories), trying to make the most of opportunities, only to be left feeling empty – again and again – was an awful trip. What a relief to be finally done with all that!"

Then, just as I thought it was my turn to speak, John pointed up his right index finger and said, "One more thing – I hope you can help Jane see that what she's been imagining is significantly worse than what actually happened."

FYI, that isn't uncommon – for a partner to assume a lot worse than what happened. I always encourage them to deal with the real stuff – which is pretty big in and of itself – instead of adding to their hurt and pain. Why do that to yourself?

Jane shook her head and said, "You can't possibly expect me to take anything at face value at this point! What's to stop you from going back to your old shit, once the dust's settled?"

John replied, "The very thought of putting us through this kind of pain is like a cattle-prod to the nuts. I've seen what a living hell looks like now ... so no interest in signing up for it ... ever again!"

I was glad to see that John got Jane's pain. But she didn't seem to get his, because the way she'd told her story initially seemed like she blamed him entirely for the marital breakdown. The cheating was definitely on John, but I knew I had my work cut out for me, in helping Jane own some of the other stuff – which is par for the course for partners who are steeping in their scalding pain.

Even in the case of addictions, although the addicts' partners don't *cause* their behaviours, they do share some similarities which can allow the addiction to grow – stuff that they have to work through.

For instance, they may come from homes where they normalized addictions, where they lowered the bar on emotional needs since theirs were never met, or where they learned to stay below the radar, to avoid confrontation.

At the end of the day, I don't want anyone to feel helpless like a victim – that's just giving up control.

That said, I'd be remiss if I didn't clarify that I'm not trying to assign blame on either party, just painting a realistic picture, so *both* parties can be actively involved in gaining an understanding into each other, that's crucial to repair and healing.

But I'm sad to say that all too often, the partner decides to stay "uninvolved" and sends the betrayer into treatment/therapy to "go fix themselves" since they themselves "didn't do anything wrong".

The reason I have *uninvolved* in quotes is, because those same people can be quite involved in blaming, shaming, berating, and humiliating.

Now I'm not suggesting that *all* partners do that, because there are many who are truly involved in the treatment process; the ones who eventually heal, rebuild trust, and end up rediscovering each other all over again – right down to the first kiss ... the first touch – in a healthier way this time!

The journey is definitely worth it, hard as it may feel at times.

To make it bearable, keep in mind that *life is about finding detours, versus becoming defeated by roadblocks; and journeying together is a whole lot easier than flying solo!*

So what exactly makes us go so far off course? Find out in our next chapter.

RECAP

- Every story has two sides – it's foolish to make decisions without hearing each other out. Healing happens when we understand and support each other.

- Each side needs to own their stuff, to avoid feeling like a victim, and to control their future.

- Understanding each other's pain is the fastest way to recovery.

- People *can* change, if they're fully invested in it. But change in response to pain or pressure often disappears as those factors disappear; change in perspective can last forever.

Chapter 2

Childhood Impact on Adult Relationships

It doesn't take a genius to figure out that the lack of communication between John and Jane was definitely counter-intuitive. Yet many of us have been there. So the question, which comes to mind is, why do we stop communicating, especially when it's critical? The answer: for myriad reasons, not the least of which is what got wired into us as kids.

Let me start with a fairy-tale, since that's where a lot of misconceptions and fantasies begin, based in unrealistic expectations which set us up. The one I'm thinking of is, the one which encapsulates the mating dance.

We hope that our significant others are mirrors that will reflect back the best in us, and not notice what we consider to be our uglier parts.

Indeed, at first, *the mirror, mirror on the wall, sees us as the fairest of all.* But when that mirror shatters, we create our own bad luck – i.e. instead of making each other feel safe enough to be our authentic selves, we start to get critical of each other, so we go back to hiding our imperfections; only this time, there is no high to help us feel good, like that initial rush. As such, many people start to fear that their partner has changed somehow – or pulled a bait and switch – and they thus become disillusioned, and may start to lose interest.

At that point, if they don't try to fix things, it can be just a matter of time before their eyes may turn elsewhere, searching for the high of lust-driven infatuation.

As previously mentioned, a lot of this has to do with what our childhoods taught us about relationships.

So allow me to give you a synopsis of how our childhood impacts our adult relationships, which may explain betrayal wounds in a way that'll help you understand why we stay or stray; and why some of us work through betrayals and come out stronger, while others fall to pieces and can never move past them.

The same event can have different results in different people – those who had caregivers who helped them out through tough moments know how to manage; those who had no-one to help them or teach them how to cope, remain forever stuck in their traumas, which can play out in horrific ways – a similar presentation to how Post Traumatic Stress Disorder develops.

Our childhoods mold our relationships for the rest of our lives – it's where our "attachment styles" develop, where we learn to do relationships, and where we can either feel safe, or have our first brush against dysfunctionality.

While it makes sense for us to want to repeat the good, what *doesn't* make sense is that we often end up repeating the bad as well.

In fact, we're drawn to recreating situations in which we were mistreated – our unfinished business, if you may – partly because we hope to rewrite a happy ending. But that comes with a huge price tag, since those pseudo-transferences carry a lot of weight with them – thanks to years of baggage – and we can end up hurting our partner, or blowing our relationship because of something our parents did.

For example, an abandoned child can become a clingy adult who'll push their partners away, thereby recreating the very situation they feared. Such behaviors stem from "schemas."

Schemas

Schemas are life-traps that keep us forever stuck in repeating self-destructive patterns. They develop in early childhood, and become a central part of our belief system, which defines our sense of self and how we perceive life, because the way we think about different things determines how we feel about them. As such, schemas are very difficult to change – even when we rationally look at something and see it for what it is, our emotional self will continue to tell us that our feelings are valid.

Dr. Jeffries Young, author of *Reinventing Your Life* – a must read – has identified eighteen schemas that lead us to repeating the pain of our childhood – a.k.a. "repetition compulsion." They include:

1. <u>Emotional Deprivation</u>: This trap represents a feeling of emptiness, so the person suffering from it tends to be insatiable in their demands, since no matter what they have, it's never enough to fill that emptiness. It stands to reason that they may cheat, because no one can meet all their demands and bids for affection.

2.   <u>Vulnerability</u>: Those who're stuck within this trap are always anxious, since they feel that catastrophe can strike anytime, and they don't have the coping skills or resources to deal with it. As such, their fears are always exaggerated, whether you're talking health, finances, safety, or life control. In relationships, they can react to a harmless flirtation like a full-on betrayal.

3.   <u>Subjugation</u>: This trap makes people experience the world in terms of control issues, where they fear everyone else is controlling their life, even when they've willingly handed over the control, in their conviction to please others. Someone in this trap may resent their partner, thanks to their own perception, and could conceivably seek out a secret affair, to regain a sense of control.

4.   <u>Mistrust & Abuse</u>: Those who've previously been mistreated or abused can't relax in their relationships, which feel chaotic, dangerous, and unreliable, so they experience anxiety and depression within them. Ironically, they're drawn to drama!

5.   <u>Abandonment</u>: Those who fear abandonment cling to their partners, are jealous, possessive, and obsessed with holding on, but they can also have people lined up as backups, just in case their main person leaves. No matter which side of this equation you find yourself on, it's a tough way to live.

6.   <u>Defectiveness</u>: People caught in this trap are overly self-critical, and they feel worthless, unlovable, and shameful, so they go to great

lengths to keep their defects hidden; thus, their inner state is rarely visible in their outer persona. Hence, they often feel like they're "imposters" and wouldn't be loved for who they really are. If a betrayal brings everything to light, these people can have an opportunity to take a shot at authentic living.

7. <u>Entitlement</u>: Those stuck in this trap feel they can do whatever they want because they're special; so they're demanding and controlling, they lack empathy, guilt, and concern for others; they consider themselves to be above the law; and they get very angry when others don't cooperate. Many addicts live in this schema, so they can justify their behaviors.

8. <u>Dependence</u>: This trap makes people feel like they can't make it on their own, because they're inadequate (usually because their parents did everything for them), so life feels overwhelming and they end up doing whatever it takes to hold onto their partner; even if it means putting up with abuse and deprivation, while they feel angry about it. If betrayed, they can often be more concerned with how they'll survive without this person, versus focusing on what they've done to them.

9. <u>Failure</u>: This trap feeds on itself, since the fear of failure becomes a self-fulfilling prophecy, so those caught up in this trap end up sabotaging themselves, by escaping what they need to do, and overcompensating in areas that don't matter as much; such as, being seductive, flirtatious, athletic. I had a client who was so afraid of

running into erectile issues with his wife that he spent a lot of time sending dick pix to random strangers on line, looking for some sort of validation. Eventually, he got caught and his wife left him – she was perfectly willing to work with his erectile dysfunction, but not with what he'd done. His comment to me was, "I screwed up my marriage... and for what? I didn't even get laid!"

10. Unrelenting Standards: The primary feeling within this trap is one of pressure, since those caught in it fear that nothing they do is ever good enough, even though no one's ever said that to them; so they end up being high achievers. Their partners thereby often end up on the back burner, and may look for excitement or validation elsewhere.

11. Social Isolation: Those stuck in this trap feel lonely, because they always seem to feel like they don't fit in, so they keep comparing themselves to everyone, and worry about what others will think, since they fear they're constantly being judged. While this person may fall prey to online indiscretions, they rarely have the confidence to take it offline.

12. Enmeshment: This trap causes individuals to be enmeshed with their partner, for fear of an inability to be happy or survive without their constant support. It often starts with parental enmeshment, which can hinder the development of individual identity. Ironically, while this trap harbors a desperate need for another, those caught within it can often feel smothered by them, leading to a feeling of emptiness, with no

individual sense or direction; so much so that they may question the purpose of their existence.

13. Insufficient Self-Control: People struggling with this schema have difficulty with self-control, containing their emotions and impulses, and tolerating frustration around achievement of goals. So they often try to protect themselves by placing a lot of emphasis on avoiding discomfort – physical, emotional, mental – at the expense of personal fulfillment or integrity. What goes hand in hand is conflict avoidance, which can create a build-up of relational issues, making the relationship vulnerable.

14. Self-Sacrifice: This schema involves people focusing on meeting the needs of others, at an expense to their own needs and gratification, to avoid causing pain to others, or experiencing guilt from feeling selfish. But when one does that all the time, they're often left with a sense of resentment towards those who they're taking care of (as is the case with co-dependency.) In case of addictions, resentment can often lead to entitlement.

15. Approval-Seeking: This life-trap involves an excessive emphasis on gaining approval, recognition, admiration, or attention from others. So one can become overly focused on money, status, achievement, at the expense of being their authentic selves, leading satisfying lives. This focus on external validation can be quite costly to the sense of self.

16.   Negativity: People caught within this trap minimize the positive aspects of their lives, and focus on the negative aspects – pain, loss, disappointment, guilt, resentment, unresolved issues, mistakes, betrayal, and potential wrongs. So they live in a state of constant fear and catastrophizing, displayed via chronic worry, vigilance, complaining, or indecision. So can you imagine what could happen to such an individual if they were to actually face betrayal, for real?

17.   Emotional Inhibition: This schema causes individuals to inhibit their spontaneous feelings, reactions, actions, etc., to avoid losing control, thereby causing shame or disapproval by others. So people end up inhibiting their "negative emotions", positive impulses, and vulnerability, and try to communicate "rationally", without listening to their feelings or expressing their vulnerability. This pretty much puts a kibosh on textured relationships, sexual excitement, playfulness and the joy that accompanies those. As such, many partners start to seek those elsewhere.

18.   Punitiveness: Those who struggle within this trap feel that people should be punished harshly for making mistakes. They have perfectionistic standards and a tendency to be angry, intolerant, punitive, and impatient with anyone – including themselves – who doesn't meet expectations, or breaks rules. Naturally, they have a really hard time forgiving mistakes, even within extenuating

circumstances. If their partner cheats, chances of forgiveness are rather low, but vigilance and punitiveness can become standard fare.

FYI, many people have more than one schema.

The good news is that these life-traps can be changed. An excellent guide for gaining a full understanding into that topic is Dr. Jeffrey Young's book, *Reinventing Your Life*. Dr. Young says that once we identify our life-traps, understand their origins, try to disprove their validity in a rational manner, and then work on breaking the pattern (after we've forgiven our parents for their own life-traps), we can reclaim our lives. The best way to do that is via Schema Therapy.

Please visit www.schematherapy.com to find a trained professional.

And here's another thing that develops in our childhood and that impacts us as adults: Our attachment style.

Incompatible styles can create the perfect storm, which can lead to a tendency to look for extra stuff on the side.

Attachment Styles

In early childhood, we tend to develop one of five attachment styles that forever determine how we become attached and how we handle feelings, resulting in marked consequences on all our relationships.

If mismatched, the distinctly different behavioral systems can wreak havoc in relationships, becoming the root of many serious problems; including one looking for compatibility elsewhere.

Thus, understanding your own attachment style as well as your partner's could very well save your relationship.

Secure:

Characteristics:

- neither overly clingy nor distant – can tolerate both connection & disconnection

- comfortable with emotions but not preoccupied by them

- can ask for what they want

- able to handle conflict without apprehension, resentment or distress

Contributing Factors:

- well nurtured by empathetic parents

- parents were reliable, consistent, and made them feel safe

Core Fears:

- none to speak of

Emotional Regulation Style:

- able to self-regulate, but also comfortable receiving soothing

---

Insecure-Ambivalent:

Characteristics:

- anxious and insecure – fearful of getting close and crushed if relationship ends
- have difficulty knowing what they want/need – and don't feel they deserve to have those met
- often people pleasers – to obtain outside validation & avoid abandonment

Contributing Factors:

- ambivalent parents flipped from rage to tenderness, so they never knew what to expect
- possibly labile mother who could've neglected them

Core Fear:

- "If I express my need I'll be rejected and abandoned."

Emotional Regulation Style:

- can neither self-regulate, nor be soothed by another (though they seek proximity) – always distressed

Insecure-Avoidant:

Characteristics:

- give up on a secure connection

- see love as conditional – feel they can only rely on themselves

- find intense emotions unfamiliar, unpleasant and uncomfortable, so try to minimize them

Contributing Factors:

- parents neglected and ignored them

- mothers took little interest in them, turned away from their cries and possibly used them for self-care

Core Fears:

- helplessness, weakness, dependency, failure

Emotional Regulation Style:

- auto-regulation vs interaction - prefer to manage their upsets on their own

Avoidant-Dismissing:

Characteristics:

- aren't in touch with their attachment needs – feel disconnected with their physical & emotional selves

- can't relate to people

- don't know what normal looks like, so tend to idealize their families

- feel shame around needing anybody – find dependency repulsive

- have a strong need for control

Contributing Factors:

- come from disengaged & disconnected families which discouraged emotions

Core Fear:

- "I will die or fall apart if I feel."

Emotional Regulation Style:

- prefer auto-regulation, to avoid connection (feels uncomfortable)

Disorganized:

<u>Characteristics</u>:

- paralyzed by conflict between clinginess & avoidance - fear both rejection & engulfment, flip-flop all over the place

- have difficulty setting limits or saying "no" directly – can be passive-aggressive

- most confusing/distorted upbringing, so have identity deficits & possibly mental illness (like BPD) & psychosomatic issues

<u>Contributing Factors</u>:

- their mothers often have a history of trauma & attachment failure, so they can be harmful to their kids vs protecting them

- inconsistent parenting can create dependency, confusion, pressure

<u>Core Fear</u>:

- "If people really knew me, they wouldn't like/love me."

<u>Emotional Regulation Style</u>:

- can neither auto-regulate, nor accept soothing from others

For relational compatibility, we need attachment style compatibility.

For example, couples who like to rely on and comfort each other, or couples who share a high need for love and a low need for power, tend to be happier together, versus couples who're unable to turn to each other, or those who share a high need for power and a low need for love, no matter how compatible they might appear in all other parts of their life.

This is why a seemingly well-matched, financially secure couple can still end up being very unhappy, whereas a financially struggling, superficially mismatched couple can stay happy forever.

When it comes to affairs, people can sometimes be drawn to those with attachment style compatibility, because they feel like they're a match made in heaven; whereas their spouse "doesn't get them at all" – indeed, there's some truth to that.

A case in point: John's straying was about a lot more than just Jane's unavailability.

John had an Avoidant-Dismissing attachment style – he felt insecure when he lacked attention, but then again, too much of a good thing made him feel suffocated.

So he found comfort in playing the numbers game – it gave him a steady supply of the former, but diluted his attention just enough to avoid the latter.

In the next two chapters, we'll see how John's and Jane's childhoods impacted their life stories.

RECAP

- Our childhoods impact us more than we realize, because we learn to do relationships based on what we experienced growing up. So any healing work has to involve family of origin issues.

- Those whose parents were reliable, learned to cope with their misfortunes; those who had unreliable parents didn't develop healthy coping skills.

- Those who could trust their parents, can let others in; those who couldn't trust them, don't feel safe enough to let others in.

- If you think someone else is more compatible than your partner, compare your family histories to see if that's based in any dysfunctionality.

Chapter 3

John's Life Story

John was the baby of his family, much younger than his older siblings. Mom adored him, dad ignored him, and his siblings resented him, because he was tied to her apron strings, from the moment the umbilicus was severed.

When John started pre-school, his life changed dramatically, because mom decided to go back to work, leaving his after-school care in the hands of his teen siblings, enraging them all the more – they wanted to hang out with their friends, but were expected to care for him. The way John described it, you'd think they sold him as a slave, and brought home his blood-soaked technicolor robe as proof of death – if they could've gotten away with that, who knows what would've happened. But what *did* happen was, they locked John up at home, by himself, while they hung out with their friends.

To feel close to mom – the only safe place he'd known – John would hide in his parents' bedroom, until someone came home. As soon as he'd hear footsteps, he'd race to his own room, so as not to be made fun of.

One day, he fell asleep. By the time he woke up, the footsteps were already in the hallway right outside the master bedroom. So John did the only thing he could do – he hid under his parents' bed. Lo and behold, he found the motherlode of dad's porn.

From there on in, whenever he was upset, he took shelter under that bed, and consoled himself with the pictures of naked women, who had the same comforting bosom as his mom – he still remembered it from their baths together, when he was a toddler.

Eventually, even the porn wasn't enough to soothe John, when his mother left his dad after learning of his affair; because sadly, John was also left behind – she was too depressed to take care of him. But dad wasn't exactly in good mental health either, to be up for the job, especially when his drinking escalated to addictive proportions.

John felt alone and abandoned, until he hit his mid-teens and met Lucy, who looked a lot like his mom, and whose eyes lit up the same way as his mom's did, whenever she saw him. Sadly, Lucy had to move, just as their romance reached its pinnacle, before they could "go the whole way", after months of serious groping and doing everything but.

Losing Lucy was the third major abandonment for John, the first two being mom leaving and dad neglecting him afterwards.

Naturally, John was devastated; that is, until he met Jane. Jane picked up where Lucy left off and life was copasetic for John once again. Eventually, they got married, bought a beautiful home together, and started to fill it with kids – three to be exact.

With time, Jane became preoccupied with other things, and John started to feel restless and lonely. So he decided to look up his old flame, Lucy, on social media – "just out of curiosity."

As soon as he connected with Lucy, all those old feelings came flooding back, as they reminisced over their first kiss, the first brush of skin against skin, the passionate urgency with which they made out whenever they had a chance, their goofy encounters, and the excitement of making their world small and each other larger than life, so they could barely be contained within it.

Before they knew it, they were both swept up in their erotic memories, and starting to feel the thrill of new love. And it couldn't have come a minute too soon for either one of them, since they were both feeling bored, lonely, unloved, and insignificant in their marriages – or so they shared.

It was all a perfect fantasy from there on in, devoid of realities and complications – that's the whole point, right? Before long, they started to live for each other's messages, via texts, emails, social media, what have you. The little chimes which notified them of various forms of communication managed to give them steady shots of dopamine – the feel-good chemical in the brain that gets you stoned – in anticipation of delicious messages. It was as if they were teenagers all over again!

John became obsessed with the affair. He couldn't help himself, since he'd come to life, even though he knew full well that he was headed into trouble – the kind that he'd sworn he'd *never* dabble with, after witnessing what dad's affair had done to his mom ... and ultimately to him. But he couldn't stop himself – it was akin to knowing that substance abuse can cause some serious harm, but it just feels too damn good in the moment for one to care.

By now, you've probably guessed that the giddy feelings were so intense that the star struck lovers had to see each other, "just once" for old time's sake.

It was to be a mere coffee, in the middle of the day, in a very public place. But there was just too much to catch up on; so after a fun afternoon, drinks were in order. The liquid courage led to an "innocent kiss," which caught them both off guard. So they decided to part ways, because they didn't want to do anything to jeopardize their marriages – as if their emotional investment wasn't enough.

And apparently it wasn't, because now all they could think of was, how the sweet kiss could've led to hot sex – long overdue from decades before, when they were left with some unfinished business. The thought became too distracting for them to be able to manage work, sleep, family; so they decided to get it out of their systems once and for all, and they were never to speak of it again after that.

Hollywood couldn't have staged a more passionate scenario, full of hunger and urgency. How could they stop their communication now, when each written line held the promises of a cocaine line, culminating in a full-on love sickness, which led to many more encounters.

The exhilaration that John was feeling infused his marriage with the excitement that had gone missing. Jane believed it was due to her efforts, so she tried to plan more and more things for John and herself. However, John missed a lot of those plans and surprises, and his excuses were starting to wear threadbare thin after a while. But he was always up for sex!

Later, we were to find out that sex with Jane was in fact more satisfying, but John couldn't give up the fantasy with Lucy – as soon as he finished his rushed encounter with Jane, and she fell asleep in his arms, all he could think of was slipping out of bed and going downstairs to have a cyber-chat with Lucy.

The lack of sleep started to show up in his poor performance at work, reckless driving, and high levels of irritability.

Jane could feel in her gut that something was off, but she chose to chalk it up to work related stress. After all, she'd grown up in a home with a workaholic father, whose addiction was applauded by the whole community, since he was such a good provider and a philanthropist. The detachment was also all too familiar for Jane, giving her all the more reason to ignore her gut; which was fine by John.

John was eventually busted, because Jane found some disturbing texts between him and Lucy. He claimed they were just joking around, and playfully teasing each other in a harmless way – no different than someone reading a romance novel or erotica to get riled up for their partner.

Jane didn't buy it entirely, but he put enough doubt in her mind that she didn't dare push the issue. Regardless, he used the excuse to break up his love affair with Lucy, since he was feeling a bit suffocated by the whole ordeal. He'd played Lucy flawlessly like a musical instrument, until it was time to change his tune.

It wasn't long before he became restless again. This time, he wanted to avoid the attachment, and just skip to the fantasy.

Cruising Ashley Madison and the odd strip club became his next thing, with an occasional porn binge thrown in for good measure.

But soon he got bored of that too, and his curiosity made him search for something more unusual. He turned to transgender porn, followed by searching for hookups with males and she-males; which fortunately didn't pan out.

Little did he know that it would all come crashing down one day, since the worst person you can try to outsmart is yourself. As Susan Cheever – author of "Desire" – put it: "It's like being the hurricane as well as the home it destroys."

Next chapter, we examine how Jane's life story unfolded.

RECAP

- Let sleeping dogs lie. If you instead go looking for trouble, you'll find it.

- If an affair feels great, you'll resent your partner for being in the way; if it feels awful, you would've destroyed your relationship for nothing!

- If you're caught up in a thrill, factor in the cost to your future.

- A fun moment eventually ends; the aftermath stays forever. It's better to give up a situation or an event than to capture a moment, only to rupture a relationship.

Chapter 4

Jane's Life Story

Jane was raised by a workaholic father and an uncaring mother.

Being the middle of three kids, she'd learned to keep her head low, and become a people pleaser – the only place where she could find any validation. It had all the makings of an insecure-ambivalent attachment style.

Among other things, Jane learned to do what was asked of her, and struggled with the word "no," which ultimately landed her in a painful place – at the hands of the neighbor's much older son.

Jane was often babysat by the woman next door, while her own mother went gallivanting – she worked just as hard at spending money, as her husband worked at earning it.

One day, the woman next door left her alone with her oldest son, Stuart – he was in his early twenties, Jane was barely prepubescent.

It started off by Stuart showering Jane with affection and attention – he went so far as to buy a bike for her tenth birthday. Jane threw her arms around him to thank him, and he hinted that he needed a proper kiss.

Being knee deep into fairy-tales and romantic stories which catered to the fantasy of being rescued by Prince Charming, made Jane's heart race with anticipation, until she talked herself into being scooped up in Stuart's arms, for a passionate kiss.

Stuart was very happy to oblige, and invited her back whenever no one was around, so he could treat her as his "princess."

A few months into what felt fairly innocuous and exciting to Jane, Stuart decided to make things more sexual, starting with forcing her to kiss him down there, and then perform oral sex on him.

Jane was horrified and traumatized, but she had no one to turn to, since she feared that no one would do anything, outside of blaming her for being alone with him and allowing things to get that far in the first place.

Stuart certainly made a point of filling her head with that, threatening to expose their ongoing "secret love affair."

Jane learned that sex was a commodity; and once she was in her mid-teens, she learned to use it to get attention, validation, affection, a sense of belonging, what have you. Some would call her promiscuous, but it wasn't about the sex for her at all – it was about what it could buy for her ... what she hungered for the most.

In fact, Jane didn't care much for sex at all, outside the context of bringing on her A-game whenever she wanted to hold onto someone.

Indeed, it played out that way with John, when she feared losing him; even though sex had been previously enjoyable with him in its own right!

When Jane had met John, things turned around for her, because she finally had a "real" boyfriend, not some closeted head-cases, who were making excuses for keeping things light.

John and Jane's whirlwind romance captured both of their hearts and pulled them into its vortex – alas, they'd both found what had been missing.

John worked hard to buy a car, so he could pick up Jane for school each day – she was the most envied girl. Later, he sold the same car to buy her a ring, since her family moved to a home that was walking distance from their school. Jane couldn't believe her luck.

Her secret scrap book came out, where she'd laid out the ideal life she'd always wanted, right down to the perfect wedding and her first home – it was the fantasy which kept her going, since it felt more realistic than the romantic books which had led her to the wrong place.

John wanted to make Jane's dreams come true; Jane wanted to take care of John – truly a match made in heaven. Together, they were going to create the perfect family that neither one of them ever had. So they didn't waste much time and started that family in their early twenties.

It was magical and wonderful, but also required a lot of them, since they wanted to give their kids the very best; above and beyond what they'd received, right down to enrolling them in various activities to satisfy their own unfulfilled dreams.

And then it happened – the disconnect grew and grew until it became a gaping hole, just waiting for something or someone to fill it.

But instead of turning to each other and doing the necessary work, they turned away from each other, with unresolved hurts.

Jane's next-door neighbor, Nick, brought her the comfort and connection that she'd craved from John (with a good dose of adulation thrown in, for good measure) – not unlike what Stuart had done for her many years ago, when they first started their unhealthy liaison.

This time, being older and wiser, Jane could say "no" to the sex, having experienced the aftermath all too often.

The incident pushed Jane back towards John, to "do the right thing." At first, it felt like her efforts were paying off; later, she wasn't so sure anymore.

Eventually, she went from experiencing the devastation from reading a few texts, to a complete breakdown from accidentally discovering his elaborate cruising for hookups.

When the Ashley Madison debacle brought down their house of cards, Jane ended up seeing everything in excruciating detail, which is the hardest thing to come back from, since every word and image gets permanently branded in your mind.

Jane felt all alone once again, as she had as a little girl, traumatized by someone who was supposed to protect her and take care of her. Where do you hide from something like that?

And thus started their journey with me, to heal, repair, and hopefully trust again.

One of the first questions Jane asked was: "Is John a sex addict, because he can't seem to get enough, every which way?"

My answer: "Let's take this up in the next session, because there are far too many misunderstandings about sex addiction, thanks to the media sensationalizing salacious details, without much knowledge of the realities and the struggles behind them."

Having gotten some insights into John's and Jane's life stories, the next chapter will explore what lies beneath their realities.

RECAP

- During moments of emotional pain, we return to the age of unresolved trauma. If your partner is acting like a child, chances are that they're feeling like one.

- To truly heal, you need to address the cause, not just put a Band-Aid on the symptoms.

- If we don't address an issue, it'll keep coming up, as if it just happened yesterday, even if it took place decades ago; the subconscious mind keeps no track of time, just unfinished business, to protect us.

- For a relationship to work, it needs work – from *both* sides!

Sex addiction is an illness where sex is used like a medication to numb out emotional pain, because it causes the brain to produce neurochemicals, which act like mind-numbing drugs.

- Rebecca Rosenblat

Chapter 5

Types of Betrayals & the Truth about Sex Addiction

What exactly is sex addiction (SA)?

SA is an illness where sex is used like a medication to numb out emotional pain, because it causes the brain to produce neurochemicals, which act like mind-numbing drugs.

It develops as an adaptive mechanism in individuals who grew up with emotional neglect or trauma.

Since SA is a disease, it needs to be treated as any other disease, without blaming or shaming anyone for having it.

That said, while the addict isn't responsible for having the disease, they still have to assume responsibility for treatment – and of course the damage their behaviors have caused.

It isn't an excuse or a get-out-of-jail-free card by any means. If anything, a sex addict would rather be free from being enslaved to the illness, versus hiding in the grips of its cage.

Some refer to SA as a "pathological relationship with a mood-altering experience", which isn't a part of a major mood swing – such as a manic phase in bipolar disorder – or the result of a head injury, or an illness like Obsessive Compulsive disorder.

Still others call it "avoidance behavior" because it's a way of avoiding dealing with one's feelings.

Addicts don't engage in their addiction to feel better, they do so to feel less.

So how exactly does this avoidance behavior get started? Studies show that childhood abuse and neglect can result in feelings of helplessness, low self-esteem, dissociation, denial, self-destructiveness – a plethora of very painful emotions which overwhelm the child, so they develop avoidant coping mechanisms, since they lack the skill set that's necessary for dealing with their emotions (nobody taught them).

At a cellular level, SA involves changes in the brain. Non-verbal relating between an infant and a caregiver has proven to be crucial for brain development, which has a major impact on the learning of emotional regulation, impulse control, and the reward systems of the brain.

When that bonding is disrupted, it causes attachment traumas in infancy, which lead to problems with emotional and behavioral control, and ultimately intimacy disorders – all of which pretty much sums up SA.

To heal from SA, childhood trauma must be addressed. As David Whyte, author of "The Heart Aroused" put it, "The part of the child that was traumatized or threatened refuses to grow older."

The rest of the psyche may grow and mature, closing like a protective callus around the wound, but the wound itself remains."

What Sex Addiction Isn't – Common Misconceptions:

SA is about quantity – i.e., if someone wants it a lot, they must be an addict. In fact, if someone has a high sex drive and a healthy way of taking care of it, sex hasn't become a compulsion for them, they can stop having sex whenever they want, and their sex life isn't impacting other areas of their life, then no, it doesn't classify as SA.

Sex offenders are sex addicts. Sex offenders are very different from sex addicts – they're into paraphilias, they can be sociopathic without remorse, or have an antisocial personality, but they don't have the compulsive component which defines addiction; yet, many people use the two terms synonymously. A case in point: Media labeling sociopaths like the "Craigslist Killer" as a sex addict.

Promiscuous people are sex addicts. While sex addicts can be promiscuous, not all promiscuous people are sex addicts – this is akin to, all poodles are dogs, but not all dogs are poodles. The reason: many promiscuous people were sexually abused as children, which made them feel debased and devalued, and assuming that their sole worth's tied into sex; so when they grew up, they ended up using it as coinage to obtain love, acceptance, popularity, validation, and so on. As such, most of them are focused on performance not pleasure, and in fact may not even enjoy sex – think Jane.

Someone who's cheating is a sex addict. Unless someone happens to be a serial cheater, or has multiple affairs simultaneously, they're not necessarily a sex addict; but it seems to be the biggest area of confusion.

Sex Addicts are bad people! Dr. Patrick Carnes, a leader in the field, clearly states that that's not the case.

Dr. Carnes says that, sex addicts can have an honor core that loves their partner, even as they end up indulging their addiction – not unlike any other addiction – because they live in contradictions and inconsistencies.

Sex Addiction is about an unquenchable thirst for sex. SA isn't about sex any more than an eating disorder is about food. What both food and sex have in common is, they can fulfill other needs, above and beyond their primary purposes of sustenance and perpetuation of the species. Try to think of sex as food, so you can understand this a bit better. An emotional eater will eat when stressed, lonely, unhappy, and possibly bored, among other things. And even as they eat their way through their emotions, they know it's not a good way to cope, but they can't help themselves, and often feel a sense of guilt & self-loathing right after indulging. Now while we can all see how food can do that – because most of us have experienced a "slipup" that way at some point – since it's a little harder to see how sex can become a substitute for other needs, let's look at that next.

How does sex addiction get started?

Imagine a child who lives with sadness, isolation and loneliness, day in and day out, trying to escape this cocktail of negative emotions, and possibly emotional neglect or trauma, but his discomfort is inescapable.

Then one day, while watching kids playing out of his window as usual – feeling deprived as always – lo and behold, he sees a girl in a window across the way, undressing.

The sight of the girl undressing creates excitement and arousal – and suddenly he realizes his sadness has changed into good feelings and he's managed to escape from those negative emotions he thought he could never escape, if only for a little while.

And every time he thinks about it, the feeling returns.

So he goes searching for more experiences like that – he might start looking for her every day, hoping she'll return, or he may turn to lingerie ads, dad's porn (the average boy encounters porn for the first time at age 11), or engage in peeping behaviors, with or without masturbation.

Obviously, masturbation provides even greater relief – in the absence of healthy parental touch that's fundamental to healthy childhood development, he's figured out a way to self-soothe with his own touch.

But since he's using his genitals to do what his heart is supposed to do, he'll never experience the right effect. Regardless, he's managed to escape very painful and unpleasant feelings.

Can you see how such a coping mechanism can evolve, where even the hunt for the next fix can create an incredible distraction … and possibly euphoria?

With time, the repetitive pattern will lead to changes in his brain, where feelings & sensations will come together to become a part of his arousal template (which generally establishes itself between 5-8 years of age).

That template, in turn, will create specific triggers, which launch ritualistic behavior that hijacks the brain from a painful place to a pleasurable place – and who wouldn't want that?

Dr. Doug Weiss, another leader in the field, identifies that as the biological part of sex addiction. He says that while all addicts have that component, only 15% are just "biological sex addicts."

When one is triggered by familiar feelings – e.g. rejection, isolation, helplessness – they seek out their ritual in auto-pilot to numb out, which makes them zone out, so *they're not all there* and thus have a hard time stopping, even when they desperately want to. This is one of the reasons that they may have huge gaps in their memory.

The other reason is, the part of the brain that's responsible for reward, motivation, and memory, changes – the former two end up feeding off each other, while the latter stops keeping score. But partners have a hard time believing that the wounding party is truly oblivious to the details they get hung up on.

FYI, erotic coping mechanisms can sometimes evolve even in the absence of sexual stimuli, because arousal is often an automated response to fear, trauma, and violence cues – to counteract stress hormones – and neurons which fire together wire together.

Furthermore, if the pairing between sex and certain emotions happens through a critical imprinting stage – i.e. first sexual feeling – the brain can be fooled into thinking that you can't have one without the other.

Once that happens, our automated thinking can take some pretty big risks when it comes to sex, if our mind makes a connection, particularly when the groundwork was laid out in childhood. In fact, trauma re-enactment is often based in recreating an exploitive situation from childhood. Dr. Weiss says that when that situation was sexual in nature, the "trauma-based sex addict" may specifically reenact that sexual trauma.

My most painful case was a woman who was gang-raped as a child, who could only orgasm while watching gang-bang porn and having rough, degrading sex. She was horrified by her need to keep going back to that, not unlike someone who's been sexually abused or assaulted becoming promiscuous; but their partners have a hard time grasping that, since they feel it should have the opposite effect.

Fantasy also allows the one playing the role of the victim to be in charge – it's happening in *their* head, under *their* control, using the power of *their* imagination. It's a way for them to mentally assert control over a situation in which they were powerless. This allows them to move forward, by creating a narrative where *they* – not the event, situation, or the perpetrator – are in charge of their lives and actions.

Beyond that category, Dr. Weiss identifies "intimacy anorexic sex addicts," in his book, *Intimacy Anorexia*. Sex addicts' suffering from intimacy anorexia are often involved in the active withholding of emotional, spiritual or sexual intimacy from one's partner. The addict may be able to share their body with others, but connecting with their partner is too scary for them; so they can maintain their distance by being busy, critical, angry, cold, distant, and dropping emotional grenades, if intimacy is expected of them.

This can be the hardest thing for a partner to understand, since they can't wrap their head around the fact that their spouse was having all kinds of sex with others, but couldn't have sex with them. Naturally they personalize it, feeling that they're somehow inadequate.

FYI, 29% of sex addicts can be sexually anorexic with their partners, while being really active with others, for legitimate reasons that were established during their dysfunctional childhoods – similar to attachment styles.

Types of Sex Addiction

(From, *Facing the Shadow*, By Dr. Patrick Carnes)

1. <u>Voyeurism</u>: Usually means objectifying the other person, so it isn't an intimate relationship, like one may have with their partner.

2. Exhibitionism: From a relationship perspective, it's seeking attention from others in an inappropriate way, with no intent of going further, just teasing – again, hard to do with a spouse.

3. <u>Seductive Role Sex</u>: Often there's a fear of abandonment, so having more than one relationship is a way to prevent the hurt that the addict is sure they'll receive. They're crippled in their ability to form lasting bonds and enduring relationships.

4. <u>Trading Sex</u>: The goal here is to simulate flirtation and romance. What actually happens in most cases is about replication of childhood sexual abuse, in which the child gained power in a risky game of being sexual with the caregiver.

5. <u>Intrusive Sex</u>: People who engage in intrusive sex, such as touching people in crowds or making obscene phone calls, are really perverting the touching and foreplay dimensions of courtship. Their behaviors represent intimacy failure.

6.   Fantasy Sex: Many sex addicts find refuge in fantasy sex because other forms of acting out are simply too complicated, or too much of an effort. It's about fear of rejection, fear of reality, and reduction of anxiety.

7.   Paying for Sex: Here, sex addicts are willing participants in simulated intimacy. They are focused, however, on the touching, foreplay, and intercourse, without the hassle of a relationship. Often, the failure is about the sex addict's inability to communicate feelings to his/her partner, or to be willing to work on his/her own attachment behaviors.

8.   Anonymous Sex: This has to do with having to experience fear, in order to experience arousal or sexual initiation. You do not have to attract, seduce, trick, or even pay for sex. It's just sex. Frequently, part of the high is the risk of unknown persons and situations.

9.   Pain Exchange Sex: For a sex addict to only be aroused if someone is hurting them, is a distortion of what goes into sexual and relationship health. Specifically, touching, foreplay, and intercourse become subordinated to some dramatic storyline that is usually a re-enactment of a childhood abuse experience.

10. Exploitative Sex: Addicts in this category will use "grooming" behavior, which is to carefully build the trust of the unsuspecting victim. Attraction, flirtation, demonstration, romance, and intimacy are all used. Arousal is dependent on the vulnerability of another.

As you may have observed, the kinds of dysfunctional behaviors that an addict is trying to enact are harder to accomplish in a healthy relationship with one's partner, since they're unhealthy behaviors.

This is one of the hardest things for a partner to comprehend – i.e., why the addict didn't turn to *them* for sex.

I'd like to end this chapter by doing a comparative analysis between affairs and addiction, so you can gain some clarity with respect to how other parties fit in; because often the injured party can't understand why someone else was picked over them, thanks to their inability to process that what the "picked" parties have in common is, a total lack of a possibility for a meaningful, intimate connection – ultimately, that's the whole point!

Differences Between Affairs and Sex Addiction

- An affair is about connection, SA is just about a sexual hit, not connection.

- SA is an out-of-control compulsion, driven by the need for a high – by an altered brain – so it's much harder to quit without proper support and professional help, even when the person wants to. Since an affair isn't about that, a person can choose to end it at any time.

- An affair is about connecting and bonding, SA is an intimacy disorder, so there's a lack of bonding.

- With an affair, there's a decrease in *healthy* guilt, which ties into one's conscience, to help bring them back to where they need to be. With SA, there's an increase in shame and *unhealthy* guilt, which *isn't* tied into one's conscience, so the moral compass has no way of guiding one back to a healthy place; which is why SA isn't about morality. In fact, such guilt and shame feed the cycle of addiction, because those negative feelings only push the addict into seeking numbing yet again; and the cycle gets worse and worse, necessitating a bigger and bigger fix.

- There are no contributing patterns in the family of origin with someone having an affair, but the family of origin for a sex addict is likely to be really rigid, disengaged, and abusive, promoting feelings of worthlessness.

Going back to John, Jane had a hard time understanding how he could turn to unattractive women, men, or trans folk, when she was good looking, had managed to get into shape, and was always craving to connect with him sexually.

"Why didn't he come to me?" was a question that repeatedly came up in session.

The answer: because John was looking to *disconnect* from his feelings, not amp them up.

Had he limited himself to a single affair, it may have been easier for Jane to understand, by her own admission.

That said, even though Jane suspected sex addiction by now, because a lot of the above stuff resonated, John wasn't convinced.

Either way, the pain of the betrayal was unbearable for her, regardless of how it panned out!

Hopefully the next few sessions would clarify things a bit more, especially for John.

We've now distinguished between regular affairs and sex addiction, and hopefully dissolved a few myths.

In the next chapter, we'll be looking at the difference between crisis management, affair recovery, and proper treatment.

RECAP

- Sex Addiction is a result of changes in the brain, in response to neglectful childhoods or rigid parenting, among other things.

- A sex addict can truly love someone and intend to keep their promises, but the compulsive nature of their illness can lead to out of control behaviours.

- Sex addicts look for detachment when their emotions overwhelm them; so going to a partner you're in love with doesn't work. Partners have a hard time accepting that.

- While betrayal feels no different, no matter what the cause, it's important to know when it's the result of sex addiction, because the causality and treatment are quite different from other betrayals.

Chapter 6

Affair Recovery as Crisis Management

It was our third session. John and Jane came in with consensus around what they felt their problem was. They were convinced that their only issue was the affair that John had had with Lucy – the rest was all fantasy play via cruising, which he controlled before he crossed any more lines. So sex addiction was off the table for them, since John had been able to stop himself easily without treatment.

As such, John and Jane just wanted to do affair recovery work. I shared my reservations, and the additional need for trauma work, but they wouldn't have any part of it – they didn't see the point – so I suggested the following five steps that are standard for affair recovery, to comply with what they were willing to commit to:

1. John taking responsibility for the affair and what it had done to Jane, validating all her painful feelings – from making her question her place in the world, to wondering about what she meant to him, to self-esteem issues.

2. John discussing his triggers, without blaming Jane – e.g. stress, loneliness, alcohol, opportunity.

3. John and Jane coming up with a game plan with me, to address those triggers and relational issues which caused the affair, so we could change the context – disconnection, loneliness, feeling invisible, lack of intimacy – the only way they'd have a shot at affair-proofing their relationship.

4. All three of us coming up with specific goals, as well as ways of reinforcing them, measuring them, and the consequences for going off course.

5. Healing and repair journey for the couple, so they could rebuild trust and intimacy.

This sounded great to the both of them, but left me feeling uneasy – I'd so wanted to work on each of their childhood wounds, and further explore the possibility of sex addiction.

It isn't uncommon for a couple to settle for crisis intervention when they first get started, so they can "get back on track" when they have no direction. But when they aren't willing to address the core issues which got them off track in the first place, I'm always concerned about history repeating itself.

And so it did – John acted out again, via cruising, *while* we were trying to work on the relationship; which was a no-no according to our contract, and obviously quite counter-productive. This time, he was ready to discuss the possibility of sex addiction; though I wasn't certain if it was his idea or Jane's, who was obviously beyond devastated and enraged. Truth be told, I was pleasantly surprised that she was even willing to stick around, considering where her mind had been.

I asked John point blank whether or not *he* thought *he* was a sex addict. True to the par for the course, he completely denied it, and admitted to just going along with Jane, so as not to lose her – she'd made it quite clear that she wanted him out of the house, unless he was going to treat his illness – he had no choice but to comply. Jane was furious that they'd wasted all those sessions on the wrong treatment plan!

Next, I asked John to take an online test – Sexual Addiction Screening Test. If it indicated that he was a sex addict, we'd work on it; if it didn't, I'd drop it.

Wishing to prove both Jane and myself wrong, he took on the challenge, convinced that he had nothing to worry about. Alas, his score indicated that he was indeed a sex addict, but he was on the moderate side.

John agreed to work on his addiction; but he was also convinced that his affair with Lucy wasn't about the addiction, since he'd become quite attached to her. So he wanted to further explore what that was all about.

I suggested that John work on his sex addiction with a therapist who specializes in just that, and Jane work with someone who does affair recovery work. Once they'd come to a healthier place, we'd resume the couple work.

But they refused to work with anyone else, since they'd already opened up to me and felt comfortable with me.

My supervisor gave me permission to move forward, with clear-cut boundaries around information sharing – i.e. I wasn't going to hold any secrets for either one of them, because then *I'd* be betraying one of the parties.

And thus began the next phase of our journey together – the part which excites me, because it's about identifying the causes, treating them, and healing the wounds; versus putting Band-Aids on the symptoms.

Speaking of wounds, we'll be looking at John's wounds in the next chapter, to gain an understanding into them, so we can address them the right way.

RECAP

- Crisis intervention can only help you through the crisis, not healing or growth.

- To change the outcome, you have to change the context which led you to the wrong place.

- All wounds can be healed, but you have to be willing to go into the painful center to clean out the wound, or it will fester and keep causing pain.

- Always be clear on your goal; if healing your relationship is your goal, focus on that, and stay away from attacking each other, particularly with what Dr. Gottman calls the four horseman of the Apocalypse – criticism, contempt, defensiveness, and stonewalling.

Chapter 7

John's Painful Past

My first session of phase two was with John. He was to draw a timeline from birth until now, highlighting all his key experiences – both positive as well as negative.

The reason he was asked to draw was because our memories and emotions live in the right side of the brain; the same side that's involved in drawing, so we can better connect with them.

It's amazing what comes up in those, even with clients who swear that they have no feelings, and whose spouses agree and wonder about sociopathy.

When people draw things, a lot of feelings spill out, making the timeline a great template for our work together.

John drew many things, not the least of which were two suicide attempts after mom left; being made fun of at school for showing up in dirty clothes and without lunch; a lack of friends because he never knew what he'd come home to; going to bed hungry; and taking care of his drunk father.

I held back tears as I watched him break down completely in front of me, over a long piece of packing paper spread out on the floor – his wounds bared open for me to examine.

The defenses which had held him upright until now, crumbled; his body folded into a fetal position without them.

It was almost as if he was ready to be born again – into a better life, because he hadn't signed up for this one. Had Jane witnessed that, she would've begun to understand the primal panic that John must've felt, when his abandonment issues had been triggered, and he started to follow a familiar course.

I encouraged John to let it all out, without shame, and reassured him that I wasn't going to abandon him as I witnessed his pain. In fact, I honored and applauded his courage. John lifted up his head and shared what a relief it was to not be judged, and to feel that someone cared.

Once John felt a bit more composed, we started to look at his drawings in greater detail.

I asked John about his suicide attempts. He shared that the first one involved him trying to hang himself from one of the beams in his basement. But the beam broke, and he immediately got busy with cleaning up the mess, terrified that he was going to get into trouble. Not once did he think that someone would respond to his cry for help, by asking what would make a young boy try something like that.

Never being a quitter, he tried yet again – the whole *if at first you don't succeed* thing – this time he took a sharp knife to his wrist. He hesitated a bit, fearing what would become of his dad, when his sister barged into the bathroom and told their dad what John was doing. His drunk dad yelled up the stairs: "Don't you dare make a mess!"

The same John who'd worried about his dad in that moment continued to take care of him, even after the fact – he knew what abandonment felt like and wasn't about to make his dad feel that for a second time.

But buying food was still dad's responsibility – he refused to give John any cash.

Time and time again John's dad forgot to follow through and buy food, since he had his liquid meals, so John went to bed hungry; his sister slept over at friends' places.

To this day, John has a hard time going out to eat, since he remembers those hardships. John also shared that whenever he feels hungry, he feels like a little boy.

On the bullying front, John drew a small boy, a mere stick figure with his head hanging down in shame, surrounded by a circle of bigger boys.

The next picture was very similar, with just two differences – one extra boy, wearing a Chinese hat, and John's head hanging lower still.

I asked him what it meant and he shared that being the smallest, he'd hoped that someone lower on the totem pole would join the group one day, and he'd end up in the middle, instead of John.

But when a tinier Asian kid joined the group and John still remained in the center, hope was replaced by shame – it wasn't about paying your dues and moving on any longer.

John had, in fact, felt truly alone – no one in his household was going to save him; not his dad, nor his siblings. I asked him to share that story with Jane.

He hesitated, didn't see the point, and then told me that I could share it if I wanted to; but he simply couldn't revisit it – it was hard enough to draw it and unpack it with me. We had to put the rest of the timeline to rest for now.

We've taken a look at John's wounds. In the next chapter, we'll be looking at Jane's wounds, to help you gain an understanding into partners' wounding, and the stages that they go through before they can heal and grow.

RECAP

- Telling our story allows us to release shame and share our pain, so it becomes more bearable.

- *Drawing* a timeline accesses hidden emotions better than *writing* about them, because drawing uses the same part of the brain as emotional memories, whereas writing does not.

- All one of us have a filter that everything goes through. Find out what that is for each of you and share it, so you don't trigger each other. For example, if your partner was made to feel worthless as a child, be aware that your upset may be interpreted as you making them feel worthless.

- If your reaction to something is disproportionate, it's likely anchored into a past wound. So try to ask yourself when you felt that way as a child, and see if you can connect the dots.

Chapter 8

Stages of Partner's Pain and Recovery

It was now Jane's turn. Jane wasn't ready to talk about her childhood just yet – she was barely managing herself as an adult. She described her rollercoaster of emotions which moved between opposites.

For instance, excruciating pain and screaming one minute, going numb and quiet the next.

I shared common symptoms with Jane. In my experience and according to my training with IITAP, it's important to highlight those, lest a partner feel like they're going crazy; or for that matter, going backwards in their recovery.

Common Symptoms:

1. Emotional turmoil – such as, tearfulness, anxiety, depression.

2. Erratic behavior, which often mimics the aftermath of any other type of sexual trauma – the brain processes the discovery as it would sexual abuse or sexual assault, and indeed it can result in similar symptoms; such as, eating disorders, post-traumatic-stress-disorder, etc. The odd time, the partner's sex drive can go through the roof, possibly as a measure of self preservation.

3. Lack of sexual responsiveness – diminished sensation, lubrication, and pleasure, along with sexual shutting down, and possibly genital pain & dysfunction.

4. Fear, which can manifest itself in self-protective behaviors – EG: playing detective to determine if the addict is acting out again.

5. Obsessing about trauma, even though one doesn't want to – the addict needs to think of their *own* inability to escape obsessive thoughts, i n o r d e r to understand their partner's preoccupation.

6. At the opposite extreme, avoiding thinking about, or discussing the trauma – a common reaction to any traumatic experience.

7. Intrusive thinking about the addiction – or acting out behaviors, like revenge, drinking, shopping – which make it hard to focus on normal life.

8. Sleeplessness and/or nightmares.

9. Emotional confusion – one can move from rage to self-blame; intense pain to emotional detachment.

10. Feeling embarrassed, inadequate, ashamed and dirty – difficulty disrobing.

Hearing about these symptoms made Jane feel somewhat "normal" – not that there was anything normal about what she was experiencing – at least she wasn't going crazy and losing her mind.

I asked Jane if she was ready to process some of those feelings, but she was just on a fact finding mission for now – things such as, what to expect; if she'll ever feel okay and how long that'll likely take; could trust be restored; was sex addiction treatable and what that would look like; and so on.

We started with what Jane was likely to experience:

Generally, most partners will go through a **pre-discovery** stage, where they know something's off, but they're not sure what that is.

They may even confront their partner, as Jane did; but the partner generally denies everything, and often ends up gaslighting them, as John did.

Once the cat is out of the bag, and the façade of the secret life has been exposed, the wounded party can go back and forth between **shock and denial** – the former causes excruciating pain and upheaval; the latter, numbness, when the pain's too much to bear. Jane nodded to indicate that that resonated with her.

I went on to say that nothing seems to bring any peace at that stage; you just go back and forth like a pendulum and get no where, as time keeps clicking by.

Even asking questions of the betrayer doesn't help, because you're not going to believe what they say anyways – the very reason I always suggest that no one should put themselves or the other party through that.

Of course the lack of answers makes people feel hopeless and embarrassed.

Where one goes from there has a lot to do with their personality, and whether or not they've suffered from prior trauma or crisis, which get reactivated and add to the distress – in Jane's case, she'd trusted her parents, later Stuart; but they all let her down.

With sex addiction, there's another huge component: the way disclosure takes place. *Staggered disclosure* – where the addict "discloses" bits and pieces for damage control and to save their skin – is the worst way, since it makes rebuilding of trust nearly impossible.

Think about it – the partner asks if there's anything else, the addict responds with a resounding no; but then more and more things keep coming out, hitting the partner again and again, knocking them over every time they try to get up and find their bearings. And even though we may be looking at the past, the hurt feels like things are continuing to happen in the present, because the lies truly are.

Not only does this multiply the partner's hurt in astronomical ways, it raises the bar on their vigilance.

Some may turn into detectives; others may retaliate because they want their partner to hurt just as they've hurt them; still others may become stuck in their pain, when the focus really needs to be on self-care, first and foremost. FYI, both the detective work (upsetting to the addict) as well as withholding information (upsetting to the partner) are based in fear of what will happen in the future, so it's really important for each party to understand that.

At the end of the day, most couples acknowledge that full disclosure was crucial to rebuilding trust – 96% wouldn't have it any other way, no matter how difficult it was.

All this was really hard for Jane to hear, because she'd already experienced somewhat of a staggered disclosure, and turned into the person who's always looking over her shoulder, and feeling startled every time she heard the all too familiar sound of chimes of electronic communication on John's phone. She'd no more signed up for that than John had signed up for the prison of his own making.

Jane rocked back and forth in her chair, as if trying to soothe herself like one would a baby. I asked her if she wanted to stop; but she was determined to keep going, as long as *she* was the one asking the questions and I was the one answering them, versus the other way around.

So I carried on to discuss the next stage: **anger and resentment**, which we agreed was pretty self-explanatory, since Jane was living it. I warned her that when it gets to be too much to process, she'll likely start to wonder if she had anything to do with it, taking her to the **guilt** stage, which then ushers in the **bargaining** stage, where one tries to regain control by offering to become a better partner. And when that doesn't work, **depression** sets in.

The only way to move past the hopelessness of those stages is to enter the **grief** stage, that's paramount to moving forward.

In this stage, partners begin to appreciate their losses and how everything in their life has been impacted by the betrayal.

At the crux of the betrayal are feelings of pain, sadness, rejection, and anger, which cut to the very core of one's heart and soul, leaving them feeling shattered and wounded. Grieving those losses propels one to deal with the pain and move beyond them. But grief isn't self-pity – which can cause one to feel victimized – so it's really important to not allow that into the mix, even as one grieves their loss of self, and loss of their emotional/sexual safety, loss of their relationship as it once was, and possibly the loss of their faith in God and relationships – the idea of being in love with someone, anyone, can feel repulsive and full of fear and mistrust, as can handing things over to a deity.

Once one has moved through the grief stage, if they manage **acceptance** via learning, they can get to the **repair** stage. All the stages prior to that can feel like a tsunami of heartache. But one can get their emotional footing at any point, hard as that may feel. Jane shook her head, to indicate that she wasn't buying into that.

So I shared that while she can't stop the waves of emotions, she can learn to surf those waves, by focusing on her own healing. But she'd have to decide when she was ready to do so. Just as an addict has to own their addiction and decide to seek treatment – no one can do that for them – no one but the wounded party can make the decision to become unstuck, and start their own journey to healing.

That said, as mentioned, a lot of partners have a hard time getting to that place; they feel it's not their problem, so the betrayer has to do all the work. This is especially true of partners who tend to be withholding, and show signs of sexual anorexia. But regardless of who we're looking at, many partners can take a long time before they're ready, and real healing can start to take hold.

Repair is marked by increased self-awareness and self-care, and less focus on the partner's behavior. In case of sex addiction, when one realizes that they're dealing with a serious illness, which causes neural changes, they can stop blaming themselves or their partner. That said, one still needs to pay more attention to their partner's behavior versus their words, stop making excuses for them, stop being in denial, confront the red flags as they see them, build coping skills, and set healthy boundaries to feel emotionally safe.

The next stage is *growth*, when one finally realizes that the issues which tie into their partner's betrayal generally run a lot deeper than their relationship – and started long before they even met their partner – so they can stop personalizing everything. One of the hallmarks of this stage is letting go of feelings of victimization and replacing them with resiliency, which leads to *healing*.

Healing allows us to open up our hearts to healthy possibilities, instead of shutting down out of fear of being hurt again. Once that fear is gone, we can feel safe enough to model how we want to be treated, by treating both ourselves as well as our partner the right way.

Ultimately, the betrayal can be used as a catalyst for change, based in what *is* versus how it should be – realistic expectations allow people to plan for a healthier future, sans the lies and secrecy.

If the couple sticks it out, learns to treat each other right, and take care of each other's feelings, they can experience a new depth and connection in their relationship.

We know now the importance of getting everything out on the table, for healing to begin. The next chapter will discuss how to do that in a healthy way.

RECAP

- It's common for the betrayed party to go through a roller-coaster of emotions. So if they go to a bad place from a good one, it doesn't necessarily mean that they're going backwards.

- Once you get over the shock of your wounding, it's critical to grieve the relationship that you'd hoped for.

- Staying stuck instead of investing in healing costs you more than it does the partner you may be trying to punish.

- The best way to obtain closure is by giving up the need for it – digging for details often has the opposite effect. If you can't find closure in you, you'll have a hard time finding it outside of you.

Chapter 9

The Disclosure

Jane's questions didn't end with me. She tried to suck John into "kitchen table confessions" – i.e. impromptu grilling – even though she wasn't going to buy his answers anyway.

I warned Jane that she'd be setting herself up for an informal, staggered disclosure, where every piece of new info would feel like a new betrayal. But she wanted it all out on the table, so to speak.

So we arranged for a formal disclosure, where John would tell her about every single indiscretion he'd had, leaving out graphic details of course – since they can never be "unseen" once they're out – along with any financial costs associated with his dalliances.

Since John had started his recovery work, he'd already made those lists, along with the excuses he'd used to justify his behaviors, as well as the actual triggers behind them. So we worked on creating a formal disclosure for Jane, to give her all the information at once.

John wanted to leave out a couple of things. For instance, meeting Lucy one last time, to give her a birthday present and say a proper goodbye, after he'd supposedly cut off all contact with her.

John swore that *nothing* happened, so he didn't see the need to make Jane's mind go crazy, wondering about that. But I told him that leaving anything out would weaken the new foundation they were trying to build – secrets have a way of doing that, whether or not they come back and bite you in the butt. The whole idea behind the disclosure is to have *no more secrets*!

It amazes me how many people want to leave out stupid minutiae, when the cat's already out of the bag, and the biggest, baddest explosion has already taken place. Why not tell the whole truth and be done with the whole thing at once? It's the only way to contain the situation and hopefully rebuild trust.

But some cheating parties think that holding back some stuff, or making light of it, will make it easier on their partner; who then ends up having to prove the lies – how unfair is that? Why do that to your partner, your relationship, or yourself?

***

D-day finally arrived, and with it mounds of anxiety.

John started off by apologizing to Jane for all the hurtful behaviors that he was about to disclose. He then went onto reading a list of things he hadn't done – e.g. illegal acts, inappropriate liaisons with people they both knew as a couple, office romances, etc. – so we could cross those off the list.

Next, he started to deliver a chronological order of what had transpired, how often, how long, and how much it cost (when there were associated costs).

Jane just sat there listening, with a deadpan expression on her face – almost as if she were listening to her accountant going over some itemized list.

And then it happened – the revelation about John visiting Lucy that one last time.

Jane stormed out of the room; I ran after her. She upchucked in the bathroom; I held her hair back. I suggested we stop for now, but she wasn't having any of it. Jane washed her face and said she was ready to go back.

I wrapped a blanket around Jane – I always keep those handy for such times, because one can get really cold when they're nervous and anxious. Jane clutched it as if it were her lifeline. I asked her what was going on and she shared that it reminded her of her security blanket – the one thing she could always rely on as a kid, for comfort; until mom threw it out.

Jane remembered the exact day her blanket was thrown out, in excruciating detail, since she said it felt like someone had ripped her soul out of her body, and thrown it out.

I put my arm around her shoulder and she hugged me like a little child. I asked her how old she felt she was? She said, "Nine – just like the day that I lost my blankie."

When we are emotionally triggered, we often return to the age of unresolved trauma. So if your partner is acting like a child, there's a good chance that they're feeling like one.

And as a kid, your problems are huge, and your solutions almost non-existent; other than deny, deny, deny – and if that doesn't work, act out.

Jane blew her nose, wiped her face, and insisted on going back to hear the rest of the disclosure.

But no matter what John said from that moment onwards, she seemed to still be stuck in the Lucy story.

John glared at me; his accusing eyes bore through me, assigning blame for what I'd caused – what he felt could've been easily avoided.

As we moved forward, Jane remained glassy-eyed, but switched from questions to comments, trying to make sense of how those moments overlapped with their life together.

Comments such as, "So when we were vacationing together, sneaking off to have sex in the pool, and you couldn't get out fast enough, you were racing off to chat with Lucy!" or, "So, whenever I'd come on to you and you had to take off for a few minutes, you were actually looking at porn, to be able to manage having sex with your wife!", and so on.

Her final comment: "I guess our whole marriage was a lie, so there's no point in trying to make sense of how things fit together."

I tried to remind Jane that falling in love, getting married, setting up a home together, having three children, laughing together, and so much more was all real.

But Jane cut in with "Not buying it. Just give me the damn numbers – as in, financial costs, *not* how many people you've been involved with."

John shared some minor costs for going online and the odd strip club; and then, he dropped a bomb – fifteen-thousand dollars for being blackmailed due to the Ashley Madison fiasco. Jane inquired when that was. John shared that it was the night before they'd left on their last vacation. Jane remembered him going off to the office late that night, "to pay a bill" when he normally always took care of those things online.

And then, when she'd noticed a huge discrepancy in their account, he'd told her that he'd bought a luxury box at the city's largest arena, so he could entertain his clients at sporting events.

Jane remembered fighting with him when he'd shared the luxury box story, since it was a huge purchase that he never bothered to run by her – of course he couldn't have shared this – it was just a cover story.

Huge as the expense was, Jane didn't fall apart, just listened in shock, and then said, "Money is the last thing I'm worried about right now, but I do have one final question that I suppose could fit into the 'expenditure category' – what did you buy Lucy for her birthday?"

I expected a costly item of jewelry, but it was nothing more than a twenty-dollar crème brûlée torch. Just as I was about to say *phew* in my head, Jane broke down and starting screaming, "How could you … how could you?"

I can still hear those blood-curdling screams as if they'd just happened.

It wasn't a response I'd expected – had I missed something?

Jane went onto say, "One last meeting, my ass! That had to be the beginning of something more intimate … is that why you stopped doing that with me?"

Who knew that a twenty-dollar item could cause more grief than a fifteen-thousand-dollar blackmail check?

Looking at my confused expression, John shared, that sometimes he and Jane would end their lovemaking sessions by putting the finishing touches on crème brûlée together, and feeding it to each other in bed.

I finally got it – it was the intimacy of the act. It was *their* thing, so she couldn't understand how he could've shared it with someone else? It was almost as if he'd had sex with Lucy in *their* marital bed … while she wore *Jane's* lingerie. In some ways it *was* that intimate.

John swore they never used the item together, nor did he ever speak with Lucy after that day; but Jane wasn't having any of it.

I asked John to explain why he'd chosen that particular item as a gift? He responded that since it was a cheap, impersonal item, he thought it was okay.

He'd also suggested that she could use it with her husband and bond over it as he and Jane had.

"You bastard," Jane snapped, "you shared our intimate details with her?"

"It wasn't like that – it was just me missing our old life together! It didn't mean anything beyond that!"

And there it was, the moment that every partner feels slighted – *if something didn't mean anything to their spouse, how could they put them through that kind of pain over a meaningless event*!

I had to interrupt with, "Jane, you're trying to understand something that doesn't make any sense to you. We need to use that emotional energy to figure out how you guys got to that place; more importantly, how to get out of it."

Jane declared that she had no emotional energy left for anything at that point.

I concurred, since I too felt completely depleted.

But John looked the worst for the wear, out of the three of us, since he had a front-row seat to the pain he'd caused his wife.

It surpassed the humiliation and shame of what he'd disclosed; the pain that he felt inside for what he'd done.

We called it a day and I asked them to just take care of themselves, physically, and not discuss anything else until our next meeting, twenty-four hours later – I always do that, so I can support the couple through the aftermath. I didn't get an argument from either one of them.

John tried to hold Jane's hand, to walk her back to their car. She pulled away.

Now it was *his* turn to race to the bathroom and throw up – but he couldn't expel that excruciating pain from within.

No disclosure can be complete without a proper apology. The next chapter will discuss how to apologize effectively, in a way that'll speak to your partner.

RECAP

- The part of the betrayal that hurts the most is the intimate details, not necessarily the big parts.

- Once the cat is out of the bag, it's important to lay everything out on the table – holding back bits and pieces makes no sense; it only prolongs the agony.

- Even though a betrayal may have taken place in the past, if you're hiding details in the present, it feels like a current betrayal.

- Just because you associated past negative emotions with unhealthy coping mechanisms, doesn't mean you should assume the latter whenever you see the former. It's one of the biggest mistakes people make. In fact, those emotions may become even more heightened, when the person is no longer trying to escape them. So make each other feel safe enough to show emotions, instead of punishing them because of your own false expectations.

Chapter 10

Effective Apologies

Twenty-four hours later, the couple was back in my office. Not sure if they'd calmed down, or if they were still too exhausted from the day before, to give off any vibes.

I tried a few grounding techniques with them, before checking in on where they were at.

When they were finally ready to talk, Jane confessed that she'd been awful to John the night before; he defended her by saying that he deserved it.

I could tell that he was willing to walk through fire, or take on the severest form of punishment, so he could move past their horrific nightmare.

If I had a way of turning back the clock on people's regrets, I'd do it! But that's never an option, is it?

And no amount of penance can make it right.

I've had people share that even a murderer is set free after they do the time for their crime, but they'll never be free of their own crime, because the pain they caused will always live inside and around them, since their crime was against someone they love deeply.

Hearing something like that often gives the partner a sense of relief, because they feel it'll keep their betrayer on track.

Indeed, many partners try to inflict punishment for that very reason; or they have a hard time letting go "too quickly", lest the wounding party think *that wasn't so bad*, and then repeat their behaviors.

FYI, the need for revenge or inflicting pain can stick around for as long as the wounded party is afraid of being hurt again.

The sad thing of it is, I've observed that the more the party who cheated is willing to take, the more he/she ends up taking, because no one is able to say "Enough!" to stop the cycle of wounding.

Going back to John and Jane, I was finally picking up bits and pieces of a shift, where they were starting to focus more on what the other party was feeling, versus what each of them was feeling inside.

It was a tiny shift, but I was willing to take whatever I could get at that point, since at least it was a place for us to start.

I asked John to describe to Jane exactly what he was feeling inside. Hearing his sincere regret and pain made Jane reach over for his hand. *Now* we were onto something.

So I asked Jane to do the same – this time, instead of focussing on her own pain, she tried to comfort John, by promising that they'd get through it, as long as they worked together. It was music to my ears.

And then, John said the magical words – "I'll do whatever it takes to fix this" – it was as if a choir of angels had joined to sing along to the music I'd just heard from Jane.

***

The next step was, Jane writing an impact letter to John, describing all her feelings with respect to how his betrayals had impacted her – emotionally, psychologically, physically, spiritually, financially, and her overall take on life.

As John listened to her pain, acid regurgitated into his throat, silencing him completely – he had no idea how every fabric of her being had been torn to shreds.

John had so much to say, but he felt ashamed; and he was certain that his words would be worthless anyways. So he became quiet and shut down.

But that upset Jane all the more, since it felt very anti-climactic to her – she'd expected his emotions to match hers; which they actually did on the inside, but not on the outside where she could see them.

Interestingly, when someone tries to read their partner's mind, they always go to the ugliest place imaginable, but rarely can they fathom the pain that might be there.

Jane became disengaged – the very thing that started it all, only this was significantly worse!

After the letter was all done, we debriefed a bit, and I made John share his feelings, which Jane had a hard time buying into by now, since she thought he was just giving lip-service to what I practically "goaded" him into saying.

Changing her mind at that point felt nearly impossible – and none of us had the energy to do that anyway – so I suggested that John take the next step during our next session.

John was to write an emotional restitution letter, which mirrored Jane's impact letter – i.e., paragraph by paragraph, he was to acknowledge her hurt and promise to do whatever he could to make things right; every single aspect.

But there's an art to apologies that work. So I made sure that John would get it right!

Key Ingredients in Apologies that Work:

Hurting each other is inevitable; so apologies are an essential part of any relationship.

However, the key problems with apologies is, there's almost always a "but" – followed by the apologizer trying to explain why they did what they did. This totally invalidates everything else.

For an apology to work, it needs to have the following elements:

- One has to hear out the wounded party – find out how deeply they've been hurt, and what specifically hurt them.

- One has to validate their hurt – acknowledge that the hurt is legitimate and understandable, and that it impacts them.

- One has to own the hurt they've caused – accept responsibility for what they've done.

- One has to genuinely repent – share how bad they feel for the pain they've caused.

- One has to offer to fix whatever they can – they have to be willing to do whatever it takes to make things right.

But while all these are important elements, each individual places the greatest emphasis on one – and possibly two – that resonate the most for them.

As such, Dr. Gary Chapman (the *Love Languages* guy) has come up with five languages of apology, which correspond to those five elements.

If you don't apologize in your partner's primary language(s), they won't feel it! It'll just sound like blah, blah, blah in a foreign language that doesn't mean anything.

And taking up the volume is no more effective than speaking loudly to a foreigner in a language they don't understand.

For this reason, I try to make sure that each party takes the 5 apology languages test on line, by Dr. Chapman.

Taking this test helps the couple find out what their partner's apology language is, so they can "speak it" in order to reach their heart.

Five Languages of Apology

1. Expressing regret.

2. Accepting responsibility.

3. Making restitution.

4. Genuinely repenting.

5. Requesting forgiveness.

Our primary languages tie into our primary needs – anything else won't meet those needs; it'll feel meaningless.

So I urge you to take the test, and then use the guidance in Dr. Chapman's book to come up with the right apology for *your* partner.

In Jane's case, taking responsibility and expressing regret were primal; in John's case, repenting and requesting forgiveness.

Had they not identified that, he would've focussed on feeling bad about what he'd done and hoping that she'd forgive him; she would've taken that as him making it all about himself, and wanting absolution without taking any responsibility or showing true regret. Take it from me, in working with hundreds of couples, that would've backfired miserably.

John stuck to the program, with respect to apologizing in a way that spoke to Jane's heart, and finally reached her soul! And not a minute too soon, because she was about to check out of the program altogether so to speak, like she always did when something felt hopeless – *her* coping mechanism.

Seeing that John and Jane were *both* still in the program, I decided to work with them individually for the next few weeks, so we could lay down the foundation for couple work, without them triggering each other.

While apologies are crucial to healing, without a proper recovery plan, one can end up right back where they started, rendering those apologies meaningless.

In the next chapter, we'll focus on "fire-drills" that help people manage unsafe situations in healthy ways; and discuss how they can be turned into autopilot responses, by rewiring the brain.

RECAP

- If you don't apologize in a way that your partner understands, where you cover the key ingredients that they need to hear, your apology may feel worthless.

- An apology must never include the word "but" because it totally negates the wounded party's pain.

- Validating someone's pain and showing them that their pain impacts you, is the only way to move past your lips to their heart.

- Making an apology is just one half; accepting it is the other. Don't negate repair attempts.

... be patient and persistent, and don't give up on yourself or your partner, just because rewiring takes some effort. If you fall, get back up on that bike and keep trying until you get it right ... And don't divert the brain to shame.

- Rebecca Rosenblat

Chapter 11

Fire-drills & Rewiring the Brain

John's work began with "fire-drills" – aka exit strategies – to prepare him, in the event that stress or shame overwhelmed him, and his brain tried to hijack him to his old coping mechanisms yet again.

They're referred to as fire-drills because they give you an emergency game plan to pursue ahead of time, versus figuring it out in a state of panic – with real fires, that can be a lifesaver, because people know exactly what to do, instead of trying to figure it out while running helter-skelter.

The simplest one's the 1, 2, 3, 4 exercise. If John found himself slipping into the wrong state of mind, he was to mindfully notice it so he could nip it in the bud, instead of tempting fate – step one.

Then, he was to vividly imagine a STOP sign, so his brain could put on the brakes – step two.

Step three was to have a vivid scene to focus on – Jane's hurt face with tears streaming down, while listening to her sobbing wounds.

Finally, step four was focusing on his own strengths and qualities, while putting his hand on his heart, and taking deep breaths – some go as far as to silently say: "I got this!" It breaks the cycle and finds a detour to a healthier place.

Repeating that exercise over and over again will rewire the brain, so it starts to seek out the new healthy detours in autopilot, instead of the old unhealthy ones.

Think of the brain as a smooth hill made out of sand. The first time you pour water on it, it'll create its own path.

The second time, it'll try to find the first faint path, since it's the only path it knows.

With time, the faint path will turn into a deep gulley, which will collect the water with great ease, being the lowest point – for it would've become an established path of least resistance.

To create a new path, you have to consciously redirect the water down a new path. In due course, *that* path will get established and eventually become automatic. But until it does, you have to keep redirecting the water to it.

A neuroscientist who works with neuroplasticity, had his friend design a special bike for him – called the "backwards brain bike" – where the right handle turned left and the left handle turned right.

No one realizes how we constantly use those handles to create balance, not just when we're actually turning.

When he tried to ride the bike initially, he kept falling off – but he didn't quit.

A few months later, his brain learned to ride the new bike flawlessly. He then went to Europe and tried to rent a regular bike, to go sight-seeing.

Well guess what – he fell off that one and couldn't manage it, because his brain had learned to ride differently.

Even though he'd ridden a regular bike the old-fashioned way for decades, just a few months taught the brain a new lay of the land – i.e. his brain had rewired itself.

When he tried the same experiment with his little boy, the rewiring took just a couple of weeks, since kids brains are constantly working at acquiring new skills, instead of resisting them.

The moral of the story: be patient and persistent, and don't give up on yourself or your partner, because rewiring takes some effort. If you fall, get back up on that bike and keep trying until you get it right – to put it in John's words, "do whatever it takes" to fix things.

And don't divert the brain to shame. It's one of the most counter-intuitive things that can mess with the process; which is why I try to get rid of it in the first session, and recommend 12 step meetings to keep reinforcing it.

I can't describe the joy I feel when someone's head bolts up from a place of shame, allowing them to actually make eye contact with me.

This eye contact is invariably followed by an admission that it's the first time someone's seen them as something other than a cheater or a loser, even after learning of their deepest darkest secrets. At that point, I instruct them to always see themselves through my eyes.

The good news: destructive behaviors *can* be changed, so we can manage them instead of having them manage us.

The bad news: many people look at all the work they have to do and become discouraged, instead of looking at the payoffs.

Some may go as far as to say that all that work and vigilance will feel like being in prison, with no freedom. Ironically, unhealthy coping mechanisms commit one's free will to a life sentence in the worst kind of prison.

Freedom begins with honesty, so an addict should commit to answering their partner's reasonable questions, honestly.

So don't get furious if your partner has a question – you put them in that situation in the first place.

And partners, if you have a question, ask yourself what's the purpose behind it, and whether or not you'll believe the answer anyway – if it's just to make someone feel bad, skip it, since that shame can push them backwards, when it becomes too much to bear.

Going back to fire-drills: they're only useful if you can hear the actual alarm – i.e. be on the lookout for triggers, so you can address them, before they create the perfect storm that can suck you into its dangerous vortex.

Toward that end, I have people write down their bottom lines – things they absolutely do not want to do again.

Next, we identify all the physical, psychological, and emotional triggers, along with whatever else might sweeten the deal.

Many of my clients identify anything from stress, to hunger, fatigue, lack of sleep, loneliness, boredom, alcohol, feeling insignificant, and so on, as key factors, which push their buttons.

Add in porn and they can become hypersexualized to the point of wanting more. So I ask them to track those things and stay ahead of them.

I had an emergency room physician who was fatigued after being on his feet for hours, making life and death decisions.

No sooner would he clock out after a long shift and his need to act out would go through the roof.

I had him promise me that he'd have a sandwich first, wait half an hour, and then see how he felt. Nine out of ten times, the urge would pass.

The idea is to have healthy behaviors replace the unhealthy ones, so there's no void waiting to be filled!

And remove temptations, so you don't get sucked in during moments of weakness – cut out of your life those people you shouldn't be interacting with.

You should also install software on your computer that blocks inappropriate sites, have your partner's picture as your screensaver, and do not carry cash or anything else that'll allow you to access your fix.

Every bit helps as you're trying to rewire your brain!

Interestingly, the very people who think those suggestions sound stupid, end up telling me that they feel liberated once they know that sneaking around won't work, so why bother.

Another way of safeguarding relationships is via healthy boundaries, which protect both parties.

Restrictive as they may sound, they can be quite liberating in fact. Find out how in the next chapter.

RECAP

- If the brain can learn a bad habit, it can also unlearn it; and ultimately learn a new, healthy behaviour.

- Identifying triggers to unhealthy behaviours is one of the key steps in controlling them.

- The brain can perceive primal needs in a similar way. Ensuring that you aren't hungry, tired, sleep deprived, or lonely, is one of the best ways to fight the urge to act out.

- If your mind keeps going to negative places, wear an elastic on your wrist, and snap it every time you go there. Since the brain hates pain, it'll learn to keep you away from those hot thoughts.

Chapter 12

Boundaries

My work with Jane started out with me helping her set clear-cut boundaries to lessen her anxiety and feel safer – she needed to rely on something tangible. It took some of the pressure off John as well, since he was really exhausted from constantly having to reassure her; so much so that his own work was starting to suffer.

The boundaries – transparency, ability to reach John within reason, computer restrictions, being allowed one question a day, and not being pressured for sex – were intended to empower Jane, by putting her in the driver's seat. Unfortunately, she took her expectations to a whole new level – of John, herself, and their relationship. There was no room for error, so even regular couple stuff was suddenly unacceptable and proof of John not caring for her – or worse, an indication that he was up to something, thanks to his last slip.

Jane's need for perfectionism spilled over into the way she started to tidy her home – it was bordering on obsessive-compulsive disorder; which isn't uncommon for those whose life feels chaotic, since it gives them a sense of order.

But the part that was really starting to concern me was, her obsession with John's recovery; which kept her focus away from her own issues, and made things really hard for John – he couldn't do anything right in her eyes, hard as he tried.

It was starting to trigger him, as it was reminiscent of him scoring in the high-nineties as a boy in school, but being yelled at by his dad for not getting a perfect hundred.

I tried to point out all the recovery elements for John, and the danger of her constantly being on him like that – it was as much for her to get unstuck as it was for him to be able to have the space to process his own wounds. But she got really upset with me, and told me she was sick and tired of me pointing out what John was doing right and she was doing wrong. Since I try to be as impartial and fair as possible, I needed to unpack whatever was behind Jane's perception, so I could address it. As we chatted, it became obvious that it was easier for her to take her anger out on me than John – knowing that, I didn't mind being the sacrificial lamb.

But I had to help her deal with her demons in a healthy way nonetheless, so I asked her what was making her rage notably worse, emotional rollercoaster notwithstanding.

Jane shared that the chatrooms and blogs that she'd immersed herself in online were constantly pointing out "all the signs" which indicate that one's partner's still cheating. So she became really confused and didn't know what to believe anymore. The problem with always looking for signs is, you can only "prove" things, never disprove anything.

I had Jane share with me some of the stuff that she was reading and realized that most of the posts were full of vitriol. So, I tried to find success stories online, since I've personally witnessed many of those – but I couldn't find any.

It's possible that those successful people just want to move on, and can't be bothered hanging out in chat rooms, or writing blogs to encourage other people, as they'd sooner put that stuff behind them.

Now I'm not suggesting that all the people who contribute are angry and enraged; just pointing out that the majority of cases can be that way, since those people are still stuck, trying to wade their way out of their pain – obviously, nobody *wants* to stay there on purpose anymore than enjoying having to look over their shoulder! So if you're caught up in that, you may want to ask yourself why you're so stuck, and reconsider what you're reading ... and why – just saying! One of the reasons I felt inspired to write this book was to give a balanced perspective!

After our discussion, Jane took my advice and started to focus on her therapy and homework, versus listening to other people's upsetting doubts, stemming from their emotions running the show.

Eventually, Jane calmed down just enough to agree to the abstinence contract, which she'd refused up until that point, even though it would've given her the space to process her emotions. She was worried that John would sneak off and try to get sex elsewhere, so she was trying to "meet his needs" on her own, to ensure that he'd stay versus stray. But the experience of sex was truly upsetting to Jane at that stage, since John touching her body was bringing up vivid images of how his indiscretions must've played out – almost like a porno flick – resulting in pure disgust for him and hatred for her own body.

If you've found yourself in that position, take it from me that sex with other parties is rarely as hot as most partners fear.

In any case, while the abstinence contract allows the time and space for the partner to heal, and for the addict's brain to reboot, many partners choose against it, since they feel hypersexual and end up wanting/having more sex than before. Others end up having more meaningful sex, where they're focussing on trying to connect, so they don't like the thought of disconnecting in that way.

So what exactly is an abstinence contract?

An abstinence contract is to give up all forms of sexual activity – including masturbation – for ninety days. It resets the brain biochemically to a neutral place – almost like having a clean slate. What's more, many couples say it ends up building anticipation; which is quite remarkable, considering that many partners had previously sworn off having sex with their cheating spouse ever again!

But part of that could also be due to recovery, which takes couples to a brand new place, experiencing that first touch all over again – which is pretty terrific if you've been together for a long time and feared that you'd never experience that again.

Jane finally understood that John's cheating wasn't about her, her body, or her sexual prowess. It allowed her to make a shift toward looking at both of their family of origin issues. No one seems to think they have issues at first – unless they were in obviously abusive situations – they just don't know any better, since our families define our norms.

In my experience, those who can clearly identify how awful their childhood was can sometimes be a bit easier to work with, versus those who try to convince me that they had a great childhood; and thus have a hard time when I try to explore certain issues with them.

These are also the people who have a very black and white, right and wrong, view of the world, where you must love your family and say nothing negative about them.

Going back to how unresolved wounds take us back to our childhood, it stands to reason that they'd feel that way; because as a child it's in your best interest to think of your parents as perfect – life feels too unsafe otherwise!

Once boundaries are in place, we can focus on healing wounds – next chapter will discuss how.

RECAP

- Transparency and healthy boundaries are a good place to start the journey to healing.

- Ninety days of sexual abstinence can clean out the brain from the impact of reward and pleasure neurotransmitters – it's like rebooting the brain.

- It's critical to find support in healthy places, versus commiserating with those who're stuck in their own pain.

- Each person needs to take responsibility for their own healing.

...I put an empty chair in front of the client, and have them pretend that the person who hurt them is sitting in that chair. They are to start saying everything they'd wanted to say back then, that had been left unsaid. At first, it feels silly; but it doesn't take long before they really get into it, releasing a lot of repressed memories.

- Rebecca Rosenblat

Chapter 13

Examining & Healing Old Wounds: Family of Origin Work

Like Jane, John too realized the importance of going deeper into his family of origin stuff.

After we completed going through his timeline, he finally agreed to do what I ask people to do at the beginning of trauma work – write letters to all those who've hurt them, listing all the ways they let them down; how they impacted them when it happened; how it continues to impact them now. The letters are never mailed; nor are they shared with anyone other than myself, and the partner if one chooses that – I leave that up to them.

In case of family of origin work, we begin with individual letters to each of the parents – which is where I wanted John to start. It's amazing how hard people resist doing that exercise – anything from "I don't want to blame them" to "they were great parents" to "they did the best they could" or "they didn't know any better." I remind them that the purpose isn't blame – they won't even see the letters – it's about giving a voice to the child, validating his/her feelings (especially when they idealize how their family treated them); and highlighting the wounds which have led to defeating patterns.

I want it to flow from the heart, so they're not even allowed to go back and read it, or edit it. If they do it on their computer – which isn't nearly as effective – they're to turn off the monitor, so they don't disrupt their thought process by fixing typos.

One woman told me that it was a dumb exercise, but she'd do it if I absolutely insisted on it. Well wouldn't you know it – she brought in thirteen pages with narrow margins and barely eligible print in a font size of six. She said, "Sorry I got carried away – once I went there, thoughts and feelings kept pouring out of me ... old hurts that I didn't even know I was carrying. It shed light on why certain things bother me about my husband."

Another gentleman wrote a detailed letter to his father, in first person; and a short paragraph to his mother, in third person. Interestingly, he didn't even realize it, until I commented on it.

Basically, dad had repeatedly wounded him, and mom had just stood by like a non-entity, never standing up for him or protecting him.

With John, the exercise felt nearly impossible. He just couldn't face how his mother abandoned him and ran away to protect herself. Nor could he fathom how his father could love the bottle more than him.

John came in and confessed that it was a lot harder than he'd anticipated; so he couldn't complete the exercise, in as much as he'd wanted to, because I'd shared how everyone who does it says that it felt like a load had been lifted off their shoulders.

But John had huge gaps in his memory, which isn't uncommon for those whose childhood was really painful – dissociation is the brain's gift to keep us from going insane.

So I asked John to close his eyes and try to remember his first home. He had a hard time doing that as well, because other than a few vivid memories, everything else was pretty fuzzy. I asked John how old he thought he was in that moment? He said around six.

I then asked John to go down the hall, look into the various rooms and find his mother. John said he found her in the kitchen, cooking.

I asked him what she did when he went up to her? He shared that she continued cooking and didn't even bother to look at him. So he tugged on her dress, but she still didn't respond. This brought tears to his eyes, since he'd idealized her as a very caring and responsive parent; which never resonated with her leaving.

Next, he was to find his father. But hard as he tried, he couldn't find him anywhere.

I then asked John, who he could go to, to find comfort – to lay his head in their lap and know that he mattered. This totally broke him, since he had no one that he could do that with. It also ripped *me* up inside, knowing how we all need someone who is attuned to us, who validates our feelings. Lack of attunement can also be an issue in families where everything gets swept up under the proverbial rug, so the kids end up believing that their feelings don't matter... that *they* don't matter.

I suggested we stop, and asked John to bring some photo albums from his childhood to our next session.

But those weren't much help either, since John felt really disconnected with the pictures.

The only thing left was to do two-chair work.

Essentially, I put an empty chair in front of the client, and have them pretend that the person who hurt them is sitting in that chair.

They are to start saying everything they'd wanted to say back then, that had been left unsaid. At first, it feels silly; but it doesn't take long before they really get into it, releasing a lot of repressed memories.

When John got into it, one of the most striking things that came out was, him crying, "All I wanted was someone to play with. But I was the only freak who never had kids come over to his house, and so I never got invited to anyone else's house either... How could you be so detached Dad, from what I needed? I'd *never* do that to one of my kids!"

John stopped, looked at me, and confessed, "I get what you're doing. You made me feel the same thing in my gut that I always felt when Jane seemed detached."

I responded, "And I bet you wanted to run to someone or something to connect with – or just take your mind off the pain."

John said, "I always did, but I should've reached out to Jane, instead of seeing her as the enemy."

I wanted to explain to John how the subconscious mind works, but our work was done for the day.

So, I asked John to start journaling his feelings, since he was finally able to connect the dots, right to the core of his emotions.

Previously, it had felt like an impossible maze that he was lost in; unable to find his way!

Once our wounds heal, we can start to build healthy mindsets. Read the next chapter to find out more.

RECAP

- You can't heal the adult without healing the child – invest in inner child work.

- If you had no one who's lap you could lay your head in, when you were in pain, carry a picture of yourself as a child and speak to it when the pain returns, with the love and compassion you needed as a child.

- Write individual letters to everyone who has hurt you, listing how they impacted you then and how the wound impacts you now. You'll never mail them – it's just to give a voice to the child to say what they've needed to say, but never had the courage or chance to.

- Journaling your feelings is a great way of tracking them and thereby managing them. It also helps you connect the dots between your triggers and responses.

As your conscious mind starts to drift off to sleep and your subconscious mind starts to wake up, close your eyes and imagine the happy ending you're hoping for, versus your fears. Utilize all five senses to really "experience" the moment. Try to do it every night – and if possible as you wake up, and once more through the day. You'll end up teaching your subconscious a different reality – one with a happy ending, so your anxiety will calm down.

- Rebecca Rosenblat

Chapter 14

Building Healthy Mindsets

Betrayal has so many layers to it, since how we respond to it has a lot to do with our history; trust issues being a case in point, since trust is installed in our family of origin – long before our relationship began, and certainly long before the discovery of an infidelity (more on that later).

In my experience, those who could trust their parents can be overly generous with giving their trust to others; those who couldn't trust their parents tend to be suspicious by nature, and have the hardest time with affair recovery.

A lot of it has to do with how our subconscious gets conditioned – this is what I was referring to when John wondered why he saw Jane as the enemy.

It was John's subconscious mind giving her that title, based on his visceral feelings – which tied into how his dad had made him feel – not what was actually going on.

Our subconscious has one job – survival. As such, it has a huge negative bias, in order to protect us – better safe than sorry, right? And since it can't reason, be rational or logical, understand language, or for that matter keep time – which is irrelevant to keeping us safe – it assumes a lot of stuff.

So, what happened 20 years ago or just 20 minutes ago aren't registered as separate events; nor are the individuals involved in them, in any given situation. And seeing that the subconscious doesn't know language, you can't speak to it or reason with it like you would with your intellectual brain. It just perceives the world using the five senses – in other words, whatever it *feels* is its reality, whether it's real or imagined. This is why both our fears and hopes – that are flip sides of the same coin – have a profound impact on our reality, by manipulating our perceptions, for better or for worse. It's also the reason why we can know something in our head but not feel it in our heart.

According to John, detachment – and the punched-in-the-gut feeling that went along with it – felt the same; whether it came from his dad or from Jane, under completely different circumstances.

The only way to work around it is by mindfully grounding each of the senses to a neutral place, from an agitated one. So I instruct my clients that if they start to feel something in their gut – like fear or anxiety – particularly if it's accompanied by a racing heart or a flushed face, they are to do the 5, 4, 3, 2, 1 exercise, to calm each of their five senses.

To start, they're to find a set of five things that they can *see* – five square things, five red things, five pictures, what have you. The entity itself is irrelevant, just grounding the visual sense.

Next, they're to physically *feel* four things – their butt on the chair, clothes against their skin, blowing air against their hand, stroking their knee – again, it's just about quieting the tactile sense.

This is followed by identifying three sounds that they can *hear*, two *smells* and one *taste*; to calm down the auditory, olfactory, and gustatory senses respectively.

At the end of the exercise, particularly with deep breathing, the mind calms down somewhat, and is less sensitive to triggering. John found this very helpful, whenever he would have a physical reaction to the negative things that Jane was saying – which happened often enough, due to the betrayals.

Another grounding exercise involves taking seven deep breaths; relaxing each individual limb by stretching it taut and then releasing it, so it feels like Jell-O; rolling the neck around until it feels loose; and then closing the eyes to concentrate on a peaceful and happy memory – using all five senses. If distracting thoughts come your way, just pretend they're little clouds that can be blown away.

A final way of controlling the conscious – instead of having it control you – is via self-hypnosis.

As your conscious mind starts to drift off to sleep and your subconscious mind starts to wake up, close your eyes and imagine the happy ending you're hoping for, versus your fears.

Utilize all five senses to really "experience" the moment. Try to do it every night – and if possible as you wake up, and once more through the day. You'll end up teaching your subconscious a different reality – one with a happy ending, so your anxiety will calm down.

In general, it's important not to feed the subconscious the wrong information, because it doesn't know the difference between thought and reality – the reason the above exercise works so well.

In other words, when you fear your partner is cheating or lying again, whether or not that's true, your mind will experience it as a betrayal. If you have that thought hundred times a day, you're unnecessarily betraying *yourself* a hundred times a day.

I totally get that you don't want to be fooled or hurt again. But if that's your focus, you're hurting yourself for sure, and may even be fooling yourself.

So how do you challenge your thoughts?

By doing "The Work", suggested by Byron Katie – more on that in a bit, after I explain how our responses work.

What causes your feelings and reactions in any given situation?

Most of the time, *you* do! Your thoughts are just thoughts, not feelings; but you can certainly convert them into feelings and drive yourself crazy, if you attach a belief to them.

When you start to believe your thoughts, they transform into unquestioned attitudes and habits, which impact the beliefs you hold about yourself, others, and the world in general. Those beliefs then determine how you react in any given situation – i.e. your feelings and your behavior – since they trigger your perception of the event.

This is why different people react differently in different situations due to their own belief systems/perceptions; yet we tend to interpret others' behavior based on how *we* react. The only constant: when one experiences suffering, it's generally because they're fighting with reality – i.e. what *is* and *why* it happened – with how it *should* turn out, how others *should* behave, and with their own ability to accept and handle the situation.

In general, irrational thoughts lead to unhappiness and other negative emotions. So if you change your thoughts, you can change your emotions. This is why cognitive behavior therapy (CBT) – a very successful form of therapy – involves teaching people to challenge their thinking and rid themselves of the *"automatic thoughts"* which lead to *"dysfunctional attitudes."* It involves recognizing when you're mentally engaging in catastrophizing (assuming the worst in a bad situation); overgeneralizing (believing that if it happened once, it'll happen again); or believing that experiencing failure makes *you* a failure/loser. Once you mindfully recognize what you're doing, you can change your thought process.

Healthy vs. Unhealthy Mind-Sets

Healthy mind-sets make sense, are flexible, logical, consistent with reality, and allow one to avoid mental chaos and suffering. Unhealthy mind-sets tend to be inflexible, rigid and dogmatic. They're based on "must," "have to," "need to," "should," "can't," etc., and don't allow one to accept other possibilities; so they react badly when things don't turn out as expected.

Here are some examples, which help to demonstrate the difference:

- <u>Concern vs. Anxiety</u>: Concern is healthy because it keeps everything in perspective, and your thoughts are constructive and solution-based. Anxiety is unhealthy because it makes you exaggerate the threat and thereby become stuck.

- <u>Sadness vs. Depression</u>: Sadness allows you to think of both the positives as well as the negatives, evaluate each of them, learn from your mistakes, and then move on. Depression makes you only focus on the negatives and keeps you stuck, which can make you feel like a failure.

- <u>Annoyance vs. Anger</u>: No matter how annoyed you are, you are still able to hear the other person out, not attribute malice, or take things personally. But when you're angry, you assume the other person's intentions were malicious, you can't see their point of view, and you personalize everything.

- <u>Sorrow vs. Hurt</u>: Sorrow allows you to think in a balanced way about any unfairness, without assuming that the other person doesn't care about you – as such, you don't wait for them to make amends. Hurt makes you exaggerate the unfairness, assume the other person doesn't care about you, and makes you wait for the *other* person to make amends.

- <u>Remorse vs. Guilt</u>: Remorse makes you think about what you did, put it in context, acknowledge the situation and the circumstances, and then set things right in a healthy way. Guilt

122

makes you feel you've committed a sin and as such you deserve punishment; so you escape from the feeling in destructive ways, and make unrealistic promises that you can't keep.

- Regret vs. Shame: With regret, you can still remain compassionate towards yourself, accept yourself, be realistic about the likelihood of negative judgment, and accept others' intervention. With shame, you exaggerate the likelihood of negative judgment and end up being defensive, avoiding others and/or attacking those who you *think* shamed you.

We have thousands of thoughts in a given day, creating an internal dialogue which can either work to our advantage or disadvantage, depending upon whether our thoughts are healthy or unhealthy, and whether or not they embrace reality.

Fixating on "if only he/she could do such and such differently, I would feel so much better" or "this is how things should happen" does nothing beyond making you feel miserable and disappointed, because it can't change reality.

Most people who are stuck are there because they can't seem to step out of dysfunctional, vicious cycles.

But as Albert Einstein put it, "The definition of insanity is doing the same thing over and over again and expecting different results."

For change to stick, you have to start to change your attitude.

So how exactly can one change their attitude? By doing "The Work" that I alluded to earlier (www.TheWork.com).

The Work

The Work is a simple, straightforward antidote to the unnecessary suffering we create for ourselves. It's not about escaping reality; in fact, it's about embracing it, so you don't torture yourself with resistance.

How do you do it? By asking yourself the following four questions and answering them with all sincerity and utmost honesty!

1. Is what I'm thinking/what I believe, really true?

2. Do I know it to be *absolutely* true – i.e. is it an indisputable fact, or just my impression? The only thing that's true is what's actually happening, not your interpretation of it, or what you think should be happening.

3. How do I react when I think/believe that thought?

4. Who would I be without that thought – i.e. how would my feelings and life change?

Once you complete that analysis, you'll be able to see the benefit in dropping those negative thoughts, when there's no good reason for holding onto them.

This is especially important when it comes to your *"automatic hot thoughts"* which spring up during times of intense stress or emotion.

They're called automatic because you don't even think about them; you just accept them, even though they're based in assumptions versus facts.

They are especially strong when your demands aren't being met – and they cause unhealthy negative emotions, such as anxiety, anger, or rage; along with reducing your tolerance for frustration, which in turn has a negative impact on everybody involved.

It goes to reason then, that such an analysis can also work like a "fire-drill" – if you can think about what those *automatic hot thoughts* might be (I feel angry when ..., I feel let down when ..., I feel like a failure when ..., etc.), you can rehearse healthy responses ahead of time. That way, the second you feel those hot buttons being pushed, you can switch your internal dialogue to healthy self-talk, and change your perception – and everything which results from it – before you cause suffering. With time, that way of thinking can become as automatic as your previous negative way.

The whole process is about changing what you can within *yourself* – with "self" being the most important part of the equation, since you can't change others; nor should you try.

Byron Katie, author of *Loving What Is*, says that there are three kinds of business – yours, others', and God's (which she equates to reality that's out of our control).

125

When we live our life in any business other than our own, we end up with discomfort, because there's nothing we can do about it.

But when we focus on our *own* life and making it congruent with accepting reality versus fighting it, we can stop our suffering!

So how do you make the change?

1. Start *thinking* in constructive ways and challenge your unhealthy negative thoughts – i.e. do "The Work".

2. Start *behaving* in constructive ways and stop behaving in unhealthy ways.

3. Repeat the above over and over again, tolerating the negative emotions that may result due to unfamiliarity, until the new way starts to feel comfortable. It's just like when you learned how to drive or dance – the discomfort and fear of the unfamiliar was eventually replaced by something that felt effortless. The idea is to keep your eyes on the goal. A hundred-meter hurdle runner keeps their eyes on the finish line – if they were to focus on the hurdles instead, they'd crash into them and fall.

4. Watch your feelings change, which will lead to changed behaviors that stick.

John and Jane both took these lessons to heart, and they both soon benefited from changing reactivity to responsiveness; owning their own negative thoughts versus what was actually true.

It allowed Jane to catch herself when she wanted to inflict pain, just because she couldn't manage her own hurt.

And John was able to pay attention to his gut feelings; follow them to their source; and differentiate his past from his present.

At the end of the day, as Maya Angelou put it, *"You may not control all the events that happen to you, but you can decide not to be reduced by them."*

Healthy mindsets promote healthy interactions – which is where our next chapter will take us.

RECAP

- Your subconscious believes whatever you make it feel – feed it positive thoughts and it'll buy them; feed it negative thoughts or suspicions ones and it'll buy those as well.

- We experience misery when we fight reality, or try to control others.

- Life isn't what happens to us; it's how we react to what happens.

- When you feel willful, try to understand why you feel that way and what it will accomplish. Getting defensive over rigid thinking never works.

For a relationship to work, it needs work – it's as simple as that; but most people expect it to do well effortlessly, even as they work hard at their careers, homes, gardens, hobbies, bodies.

- Rebecca Rosenblat

Chapter 15

Healthy Interactions

As I'd shared before, when I do betrayal work with a couple and help them reach a better place than they ever thought possible, they invariably share some version of this statement: "Twisted as it sounds, this was the best thing that happened to us, because it was a wakeup call that made us cherish our relationship and work on it."

While I'm thrilled to hear that they've finally found their sweet spot, it always breaks my heart that something bad had to happen for these people to cherish their relationship and do the necessary work.

For a relationship to work, it needs work – it's as simple as that; but most people expect it to do well effortlessly, even as they work hard at their careers, homes, gardens, hobbies, bodies.

Whatever happened to the person who wondered if they were noticed by that special someone; if they'd ask them out, or respond favourably to being asked out? Then came the first date, with all the nervous butterflies, working on making a great impression, plus or minus million wardrobe changes that mimic the multiple outfit sequence in rom coms, complete with perfect background music.

From there, it might've been a bit of a waiting game – wondering if there will be future dates ... a steady relationship ... a commitment of sorts ... possibly marriage or co-habitation ... maybe kids ... a bigger and better home ... and so on.

What amazes me is, at some point, people go from that anticipation and longing for their beloved, to taking them for granted, to possibly wounding them; and from only seeing the best in them to imagining the worst in them, ascribing horrific intent.

In some cases, the latter is to create an entitlement to move onto something else; in other cases, it's personal insecurities causing a negative projection onto the partner; in still other cases, it's seeing them through unresolved wounds of the past – if the magnitude of your reaction to a situation is disproportionate, you can bet it's anchored in your past.

John and Jane were no different. They couldn't believe their luck when they found each other, became soulmates, and then decided to create a new family that was very different from each of their families of origin, which spelled a lot of pain for the both of them. But then, true to the hallmark of human nature – repetition compulsion – they allowed their old unresolved wounds and coping mechanisms to take over, and destroyed the very thing that was most sacred to them.

I realize that it was John's betrayal that led them to my office, but there was a lot more that happened to erode the relationship, long before that.

It is said, if you want to destroy a relationship outright, have an affair; if you want to slowly bludgeon it to death, start neglecting, nagging, withholding, ignoring – well, you get the picture.

Now I don't know about you, but personally, I'd hate to be slowly bludgeoned to death. Point being, we each need to own the part we play in the marital breakdown, even if it may just be enabling and codependence, which can easily be mistaken for support.

By definition, codependency means making the relationship more important than yourself. It can be one-sided, because one party is trying to make the relationship work, with someone who may have checked out. When the less invested party behaves badly, the codependent party tries to put up with them, or fix the situation. It could be the result of them feeling that they're not good enough, so they have no choice but to put up with it; or because that dynamic makes them feel like they're the better person, so it helps their poor sense of self – and possibly makes them feel that they'll eventually be recognized and/or rewarded for their hard work, because they rely on the other party to feel good about themselves.

FYI, not all partners are codependent. Many are strong, have a very healthy sense of the self, maintain good boundaries, don't self-blame, and are highly functional – emotionally, professionally, spiritually.

Codependency symptoms are common in (but not limited to) people who grow up in dysfunctional homes – they get used to pain, conflict, and dealing with emotionally disengaged individuals, so they accept those things from their partners, whereas others may not.

But accepting doesn't mean that they hurt any less; or for that matter, that they aren't triggered by them. I'd wondered if that's what was going on with John, but wasn't certain just yet.

So, how do you know if *you're* in a codependent situation? Ask yourself the following three questions:

1. Is this relationship more important to me than I am?

2. Am I paying a high price for being with this person?

3. Am I the only one putting energy into this relationship?

To check if you have a tendency towards codependent relationships in general, see if you display one or more of the following patterns:

*   People pleasing – giving too much in relationships.

*   Avoiding conflict.

*   Relying on others for defining self-worth.

*   Having poor boundaries.

*   Ignoring red flags.

Interestingly, even smart, successful, self-reliant individuals can end up in codependent situations.

I've worked with many people at the top of their game professionally, but when it came to their relationships, all that self-assuredness went out the window. If any of this resonates, it's important for one to do a mental inventory, to determine if they believe love is supposed to be painful, because of what they saw growing up. That being the case, people can self-sabotage their chances of having a healthy relationship, where they can get their needs met, versus confusing drama and intensity with intimacy.

Unless one owns that part and works on it, they're just as responsible for unhealthy relationship patterns as the partner they blame.

That said, even those who repeatedly end up in the latter scenario may eventually get to the point where they feel they've had enough – and that can be the moment which nudges them towards healthy change... The willingness to leave, is often what sets things straight at that point. But it has to be a genuine effort to want better for oneself, not a game where one hopes they'll make the other person miss them – or teach them a lesson, for that matter – because it's still about the other party in that case.

As a sidebar, codependent individuals are often drawn to troubled, distant, or moody people, and can't tear themselves away from them – despite being treated badly by them – but they can dismiss "nice" candidates as "boring." Eventually, their unhealthy situation makes them spiral down, because nothing erodes self-esteem quicker than an unhealthy relationship. The good news: codependent individuals *can* heal, reclaim their lives, and end up in healthy relationships, if they:

- Visualize themselves in loving relationships which meet their needs – mindfully experience what that looks like, using all five senses. As mentioned before, this is especially great when done at bed-time, when the subconscious mind is ready to be reprogrammed (as our sleep takes our mind into the beta-theta waves zone).

- Challenge their beliefs and self-defeating thoughts about their self- worth, every time they pop up in their head – Cognitive Behavior Therapy can really help with that.

- Be kind and compassionate towards themselves. It's healthy to accept help when needed – seeing a therapist could be a game-changer.

- Not allow their fear of rejection to stop them from achieving loving, intimate relationships. Being drawn to broken people to minimize rejection is nothing more than faulty, self-defeating thinking; and FEAR is no more than **F**alse **E**xpectations **A**ppearing **R**eal!

For more information on addressing codependence, I highly recommend Melody Beattie's book, "Codependent No More".

Back to John and Jane. John had tried to hang on, without expressing his needs and wounds; and then when things got rough, he'd taken the back door out of his relationship into self-soothing.

As well, since he had a hard time expressing his anger and disappointment in healthy ways, he engaged in passive aggressive ways, which drove Jane nuts, and made her just ignore him all the more when he acted that way.   And that ignoring looked a lot like disengagement to John. ... Can you see where I'm going with this? If you guessed *creating a vicious cycle*, you're absolutely right.

When we see repeating patterns, we need to take an inventory – possibly via journaling – to identify our triggers and follow them to their source.

In John's case, he realized that he couldn't stand up to Jane, for fear of abandonment; so he managed his negative emotions by subconsciously "punishing" her, while trying to make himself feel better.

134

This doesn't imply by any means that Jane was off the hook; because she too used anger and disengagement instead of trying to find out what was really going on, when things felt off. FYI, often people use anger to control their feelings, as long as they fear getting hurt. And the way they express it might be reminiscent of how they wanted to express it as a child but couldn't; which also ties into wanting to have some control – over the situation in this case.

After we looked at what each of them brought to the table, John was finally able to see the woman he married, versus the "angry, cold bitch" he'd turned away from.

He also tried to take ownership for possibly turning her into that woman. But Jane was quick to jump in with, "I too could've chosen to fix things, instead of turning into that woman that neither one of us liked very much."

John said, "But you *did* try, when you worked hard to look better, and made an effort to be more intimate with me. I'd just turned to Lucy by then."

Jane responded, "All that effort was focussed on winning you back, not figuring out why you pulled away in the first place, because I'd have to own *my* part in that."

And that was the second shift they showed, which excited me to no end. They were now ready to work through the causes of the breakdown that they'd both identified and owned, versus settling for Band-Aid solutions like the time they just wanted to focus on crisis management and affair recovery.

Looking at our pasts feels painful; change feels downright scary; giving up old habits and things that we no longer use/need feels nearly impossible.

We have a hard enough time throwing out old CDs, even when our car/home may no longer have a CD player; throwing away coping mechanisms is a million times harder, even though it's armour that's doing nothing more than weighing us down.

The best thing you can do for yourselves is, get rid of the baggage that came between the two of you, change the context which hurt you, lose the coping mechanism that's no longer serving you, and build a heathy, safe haven together.

You have more impact on each other than you might realize. According to Dr. Sue Johnson, author of "Hold me Tight", our primal panic kicks in when we're severed from our beloved; but having them by our side makes everything bearable. Put another way: suffering is inevitable; suffering alone is unbearable.

One of the most revolutionary studies on the subject matter placed sixteen females in an MRI machine and told them that they were going to get a shock on their ankles, each time they saw a cross.

In the first group, they lay there all alone – both the anticipation of the pain as well as the pain itself were experienced rather harshly.

In the second group, a stranger held their hand – the pain was more bearable, but still hurt. In the final group, each woman's hand was held by her husband's hand – neither the pain nor the anticipation felt too bad at all.

What this study demonstrated was that when we feel alone, our pain – physical or emotional – becomes unbearable; when we're together, it doesn't feel nearly as bad. This is also true of healing.

The moral of the story: you're better off journeying together, instead of going it alone, because you feel you can't be vulnerable together. Yes, it can be scary; but as long as you're both all in, you're on the same side – i.e., disinterested in jeopardizing the relationship.

So take each others hand, let each other in, and make each other feel safe enough to be authentic. Sure beats the alternative, where the very thing you're trying to safeguard yourself against – pain – takes over in unbearable ways!

One of the things that can prevent healthy interactions is fear, by making us react in counterproductive ways. Find out more in the next chapter.

RECAP

- If your beliefs aren't serving you the right way, they're hindering you – so challenge them.

- Try to remember what brought you together, what has kept you together, and the strengths that will help you get through this.

- Suffering is a given; suffering alone is unbearable; so support each other the best way you can manage.

- We impact each other in tremendous ways – always think about what kind of impact your words will have on your partner; and if it's consistent with what you're hoping to accomplish.

Many betrayed parties get stuck in the saying: 'Fool me once, shame on you; Fool me twice, shame on me!'
- Rebecca Rosenblat

Chapter 16

When Fear Takes Over

John and Jane were finally starting to turn things around. They were having normal conversations, with lesser and lesser stuff around the betrayal; whereas previously, everything was about just that.

It was time for their first big date night, since their relationship blew up. John had planned an entire day – golfing, dinner, theater, dessert! Jane couldn't be more excited.

Since this was right after their ninety days of abstinence, Jane decided to give intimacy a shot as well, as a surprise to mark the grand finale for their big date.

Normally, I have couples ease back into it with "sensate focus" – two weeks of just kissing and making out with clothes on, like teens do; two weeks of fooling around without clothes, but the genitals are strictly off limits; two weeks of allowing genital play as part of sensual touching, but penetration is off the table; and finally doing whatever comes naturally. The idea is to rediscover each other, build anticipation, and finally bring everything together for a holistic experience

But Jane wanted to go straight for the forbidden fruit, since they were in a good place emotionally, and they were both yearning to be physically close to each other.

So at the end of their lovely evening, Jane said that she

was going to have a sumptuous bath, and John was welcome to join her if he wanted to.

While Jane ran the bath, she decided to put on some soft music on John's iPod. Just as she was scrolling through his playlists, a text appeared, from Lucy:

Hey sexy ... Miss me? ;)

Obviously, Jane was mortified ... devastated ... crushed! She wanted to confront John but thought better of it, because she wanted to give him a chance to come clean on his own – a part of her had hoped that this was a one-sided, isolated incident that he'd share with her.

Jane wiped her tears, set aside the iPod, and slipped into the bath, covered right up to her neck in foamy bubbles – the thought of being naked in front of John felt awful, considering the circumstances.

John rushed up the stairs with two glasses of wine, strawberries, and whipped cream, practically salivating at the thought of things to come. He set them on the marble step next to their deep bathtub, and slipped into the bath with Jane.

The thought of their naked bodies coming together in any capacity – with what had just transpired – nauseated Jane, but she had to stick to the plan.

That said, bathing together was one thing, having sex quite another. So Jane feigned being tired and called it a night, after their bath and drinks were done.

Jane fully expected John to hop on his iPod at that point – or at the very least, check his smart phone for messages. But John followed her into bed. Part of her was really happy that he'd rather spoon up into her – even when sex wasn't in the cards – versus catch up with his messages, which he'd ignored the entire day. But another other part had wanted John to check his messages and pass or fail her test right away, so she wouldn't have to spend another restless night wondering – she'd done that far too many times in the past.

Next morning, John got up, brought Jane breakfast in bed, and they both checked their texts and emails. He had to have seen Lucy's message by now. So Jane leaned over and casually asked, "Anything interesting?"; John replied: "Nothing worth mentioning."

Nothing worth mentioning? Jane was horrified that he was keeping secrets from her yet again. She figured, there had to be only one reason – the affair was still ongoing and he didn't want to be found out. She saw red with rage and couldn't think of anything else.

But she wanted to drop the bomb in our session the next day, so I'd witness his expression when she caught him by surprise – quite different from the surprise she'd initially intended.

***

The next day, before I could do a check-in with John and Jane, or ask them to catch me up on their week, Jane said, "I think John has something to tell us."

John looked puzzled, and said, "I do?"

Jane said, "You tell me – unless you think a text from Lucy is no big deal ... maybe it's so commonplace that it didn't even register!"

John became pale and just glared at Jane. She hissed, "Go ahead, flip it around on me ... as in, I had no right to snoop ... you have a right to your privacy ... whatever."

I'd recommended that either one of them could ask to see the others electronic devices at any point, without notice; but snooping around doesn't help either party – as I'd said before, you can't disprove anything that way, so the anxiety remains, and you try harder and harder to find something.

John finally responded, "I wasn't going to say that at all. The text was a stupid one off thing – the second I read it, I texted Lucy to never contact me again, and blocked her on everything, including social media. So, since I thought that I'd already taken care of it, I didn't see the need to burden you with it; or set you back after how far we've come."

And that right there is the mistake that many people make. They think that sharing something like that will set their partner back.

In fact, it has the *opposite* effect; because while it'll no doubt be upsetting, it shows a commitment to the truth – sharing something that may never have been found out otherwise. ... It is *those* very moments that build trust!

That said, most people have John's reaction, when they think they did nothing wrong; and get sick of being accused for the same reason.

The wrong decision set Jane back by a few months. She wasn't buying that it was an isolated incident, where she just *happened* to be in the right place, at the right time, to catch it. Had John volunteered that information, she would've likely believed him.

So I talked about the importance of making each other feel safe enough to be honest, hard as that might be.

John looked up at her, with tears welling up in her eyes, and said, "I can't believe I blew it again. But you have to believe me when I tell you that it was honestly just that one time, and I've blocked her on every device, since. ... Please, Jane, at least entertain that possibility."

Jane said, "No can do – after everything we've gone through, *this* is how you pay me back, by slipping up yet again? I gave you a second and a third chance, but no more – I'm done! ... I guess once a cheater, always a cheater!"

I had to call a time-out and ask John to explain why he was so afraid of telling Jane, if nothing was going on, on *his* side?

John shared another incident, where he'd insisted they leave a gathering because he'd spotted Lucy in the crowd. Jane had a hissy fit and accused him of wanting to hide, because he was probably still seeing Lucy and didn't want to be seen with his wife.

Jane had also gone on to say, "Why do I have to change my life because of that bitch? I'm staying exactly where I am, on your arm ... thank you very much!"

Fortunately, Lucy had left with her husband, when she saw John and Jane.

It was a teaching moment: I was able to point out the importance of allowing one to feel safe enough to share the truth. I was hoping that Jane could entertain at least the *possibility* of John telling the truth, even though he hadn't been forthright at get go; based on the whole once bitten twice shy thing.

But John had checked out at that point; his head hung down in shame, looking defeated.

I asked John what he was thinking. He said, "This will never be over, will it? I'm constantly afraid of something happening that I'll have to pay for. Then again, I guess I deserve it, because of what I did. Jane was never as suspicious or caustic as she is right now. Maybe we'd be better off living separately."

Jane barked, "So *that's* what you want? ... Do you honestly think that I enjoy being this person who's constantly looking over her shoulder?"

John blew out a frustrated breath, looking hopeless, sad, beaten, full of shame.

It was clear that there wasn't anything that John could've said to reach Jane at that time – and I too was feeling that way. I was caught between wanting to help them set things right and worrying that I'd lose Jane once again, as I had before.

So I did what any therapist would do – I insisted that they turn to and look at each other, and share from their heart, what they were really feeling, and possibly fearing; and then we'd call it a day.

Watching his pain, I saw a glimmer of hope in Jane's eyes. But she wasn't ready to drop it just yet; since that would make her vulnerable, and unable to trust herself.

Many betrayed parties get stuck in the saying:

Fool me once, shame on you;

Fool me twice, shame on me!

Since being stuck often means unresolved trauma, I had to leave it for now – at least they heard each other out, and unlike the last time, Jane took John's hand when he offered it to her this time, as they left the session.

Just as John and Jane were getting to a good place, her fears catapulted her mindset to the worst place possible.

Will she ever be able to rebuild trust? Is it even possible to rebuild trust?

Read the next chapter to find out – it'll be one of the most crucial chapters thus far!

RECAP

- Challenge your thoughts before they become your beliefs – it's hard to fight those.

- Getting caught up in what-ifs makes you focus on things that may *never* happen, instead of working on what *is* happening.

- Always look for other possible explanations versus those that are closely connected to your fearful filter. People think being suspicious will somehow protect them; when it does more harm than good.

- Trust is a fragile thing – it can't tolerate too many hits.

It is said that through their allegiance to you, your girlfriends can talk you out of a perfectly good marriage/job/home.

- Rebecca Rosenblat

Chapter 17

Rebuilding Trust

As Jane withdrew from John, she started to confide in Nick more and more, using him as a crutch yet again, even though deep down she knew that wasn't going to help one bit.

After a while, Nick started to want more than Jane was willing to give, just like before. Keeping that a secret from John told her in her gut that she was no better than him, so she decided to open up to her two best girlfriends – Cynthia and Laura – to ask for their input.

I couldn't have picked a better duo myself, because while Cynthia constantly filled Jane's head with how she could *do* so much better, how she *deserved* way better, how guys would be lining up to date her and treat her right; Laura painted a more realistic picture. Laura had been in the dating scene, post-divorce, far too long, so she was more grounded in reality.

It is said that through their allegiance to you, your girlfriends can talk you out of a perfectly good marriage/job/home. Cynthia was definitely one of those. But Laura balanced everything out. It was almost as if Cynthia was saying what Jane must've wondered – but was afraid to ask – and Laura was addressing everything oh-so-proficiently.

Laura pointed out that if Jane were to leave, their lifestyle would take a nosedive, in maintaining two households instead of one; that most guys their age who're getting out of bad marriages only want to have a good time, not jump into another relationship; and most important of all, since John already loved her and had lived through the pain of brokenness with her, he was less likely to do anything like that again, versus someone new that she had no history with.

Having heard hundreds of stories myself, I would agree with Laura, for the most part – of course there are exceptions to every rule on the former, but not so much on the latter.

Not meaning to sound bleak, but there are *no* guarantees that the next guy won't hurt you, since they bring their own baggage – so no such thing as a fresh start, even if they had been cheated upon and thus promised that they'd never do that to you. I'm by no means suggesting that everyone will hurt you; just recommending that if you think your being hurt is the only reason you want to pull the plug on your current relationship, think again!

Furthermore, the sense of comfort that you feel with your husband of many years – the father of your children – is very different from anything you can put together in a blended family, where there's always some sense of yours versus mine; and the second wife rarely gets treated as well as the first one. But that's not to say that you stay in a bad situation by any means.

Now before we go any further, since we're trying to clarify a few things, I want to clarify that outside of sex addiction – and possibly the early stages of playing the field – one rarely goes *looking* for an affair. It kinda sneaks up on you.

You may stop feeling special at home and then someone makes you the center of their universe, and you get sucked into that vortex. And before you know it, you're relying on them to feel good. In some cases, it remains an emotional affair, in other cases, it's a matter of time before the skin-to-skin line is crossed. So what exactly is an emotional affair? Here are some leading indicators:

7 Signs That You Are Having an Emotional Affair:

1. You invest a lot of emotional energy into this person, by sharing stuff – such as hopes and dreams – that you don't even share with your partner (even though such sharing would help you actually connect with them).

2. You dress up for this person.

3. You find ways to spend time together, which becomes very important to you.

4. You'd feel guilty if your partner saw you together, because you're saying or doing things that you wouldn't say or do in front of them. FYI, I always tell my addicts that *all* their interactions should pass that test – and they love having that clear-cut boundary to keep themselves in check!

5. You might share your feelings of marital dissatisfaction with them.

6. You keep secret the amount of time you spend with this person, including emailing, calling, and texting.

7. You start to depend on the emotional high that comes from that relationship.

Incidentally, even one or two of these signs count.

Beyond that, the digital world that lives between fantasy and reality can also cause a lot of confusion, because often, you don't even meet those people for real.

And there are no rules as of yet; so everyone has their own impression of what's right and wrong.

The therapeutic definition of an affair is, anything, which takes emotional or sexual energy away from the primary relationship – could be cyber stuff, porn, a close friendship, what have you.

Often – but by no means always – the betrayed partners can cross one of those less obvious lines themselves, but they hold onto the self-righteous stance which goes something like this: "I was also very unhappy, but I didn't do to you what you did to me."

Or, they can be withholding, cold, rejecting, critical, punishing, or disengaged; but they don't want to take any responsibility for their own coping mechanisms.

Bottom line, instead of splitting hairs, the focus should be on both parties trying to heal the wounds that they've caused each other, and moving forward to create a new context, where the relationship becomes a priority.

When I discussed those things with Jane, oddly enough, she didn't argue with me this time; just tried to convince me that what John had done was significantly worse.

I didn't debate Jane's point – obviously her hurt was significantly deeper than his – but I just wanted Jane to take some responsibility, instead of playing the victim; because what we can't own, we can't change.

That said, it was a while before Jane got back on track, after waging a cyber war on Lucy, over social media. She practically stalked and humiliated her, until Lucy started to play tricks on Jane's mind, by feeding her lies, just to get back at her. Jane had given Lucy complete control over how she was feeling. Lucy could make anything up and she would play right into her hands, by buying it, grilling John, and widening the rift between them. When I helped Jane see that she was giving Lucy way too much power over their relationship, Jane finally backed off.

But Jane didn't stop there – she opened up a fake account to try and seduce John online next, to "test" him. However, John never took the bait – not that he knew it was her; he just wasn't interested.

After that, Jane tried yet another trick – she hired a honeypot to flirt with John at the bar at his tennis club, to see how far he'd go. Again, it was a no-go.

Finally, Jane turned to John, ready to work on rebuilding their relationship again. John was truly hurt by the exorbitant extents she went to, trying to entrap him; but he was glad that it finally gave her some peace of mind.

Unlike John, most betrayers end up saying, "You either trust me or you don't," which isn't reassuring by any means, since their partner has no way of knowing what's inside their head; even when they themselves know they are no longer doing anything wrong. So it's important not to lose sight of that.

For the above reasons, I try to offer partners a greater understanding into trust, so they can healthily assess their situation on their own, instead of interrogating someone they're not going to believe anyway.

Trust

(Some comments from David Richo's book, "Daring to Trust" – a must read!): Trust is the foundation of all human connections, which makes it one of the most important aspects of romantic relationships – it's the glue which holds them together. Breakdown in trust is thereby a lot more painful than a breakup of a relationship. But whether or not we're able to trust someone doesn't start the moment the relationship does, or for that matter the moment a betrayal is discovered. Trust has a history behind it. So it's very important that we explore our own history.

Think back on all the major people that have impacted your life, from your childhood until now. Ask yourself if you've fully appreciated what each person brought to your history of trust – for better or for worse. When it was for worse, did you actually deal with it, or are there past hurts and mistrusts that are still unresolved?

To access that connection, think of all the feelings a current betrayal has roused in you; assuming that's why your trust issues have resurfaced again. Did you feel any of those feelings before at any other point in your life? If so, what you're feeling in your current situation could be anchored down by the heavy weight of all the past broken trusts, especially if they haven't been dealt with. Ultimately, trust happens in the present, but it connects past experience with future probability.

Richo says that we need to look for the five 'A's if we're worried about infidelity – if they're present, we can more than likely trust that person. The five 'A's are: **A**ttention, **A**cceptance, **A**ppreciation, **A**ffection and **A**llowing – as in, allowing one to show their feelings without being interrupted, punished, or ridiculed; giving one the permission and encouragement to live in accord with their deepest values and healthy needs; and protecting and supporting one's healthy dreams. As you ensure that those ingredients are present in your relationship, trust will grow. It's nearly impossible for someone to express those five elements, and genuinely be there for us, if their attention is elsewhere.

When people look back at the times when their partner was acting out, they can identify that those five 'A's were generally missing – it's a major "aha moment." Richo says the five 'A's are replaced by other behaviours when one's ego becomes more important than their partner. FYI, an isolated behaviour or two mustn't be looked upon as "diagnostic," as most of those can occur for other reasons. It's only noteworthy when the 5 As are consistently replaced by the following behaviours:

Attention to a partner is replaced by *Self-Absorption.*

Acceptance of a partner is replaced with *Judgment & Criticism.*

Appreciation for a partner is replaced by *Indifference or Blame.*

Affection for a partner is replaced by *Distancing.*

Allowing a partner to pursue their values and dreams is replaced by *Controlling.*

Jane totally got that. I also reminded her that trust isn't just about fidelity. If she could trust John to be there for her; come when she called/needed him; take care of the kids with integrity; not blow their money like those who commit fiscal infidelity; and be willing to do the work that's needed; then her overall trust in him could act as a foundation for rebuilding broken parts of her trust. But while that sounds good in theory, rebuilding trust is one of the hardest things, and without it, pretty much everything else can backfire – partners keep slipping into suspicious places.

Their constant state of fear can cause depression, weight gain, poor concentration, and a diminished sense of self. Dr. Doug Weiss believes in doing a polygraph at get go, with disclosure, so the partner has peace of mind. He does it as a baseline intensive. In his experience, partners often learn reality is somewhere between what they know and what they fear (for more information on this, please visit: http://drdougweiss.com/intensives). At the end of the day, you need to do whatever it takes to rebuild trust – come at it in different ways, if need be! With trust, comes intimacy, with all its challenges – the focus of the next chapter.

RECAP

- Any action which takes away emotional or sexual energy from your primary relationship counts as an affair.

- Trust isn't just about sexual fidelity; it's about being able to rely on each other to be there, and treat each other right.

- Look for the 5-'A's, which demonstrate that someone is invested in you, versus someone else. They are, **A**ttention, **A**cceptance, **A**ppreciation, **A**ffection and **A**llowing – as in, allowing one to show their feelings without being interrupted, punished, or ridiculed.

- Trust is a two-way street; if someone is trying to be trustworthy, do what you can to be trusting.

Chapter 18

Intimacy Challenges

I guess you're wondering about whatever happened with intimacy with John and Jane?

After our pep talk on trust, Jane took the bull by the horns one day, and decided to plan a special evening, before she lost her nerve. She cooked John's favourite meal – eight-layer lasagne – and waited for him to come home; she'd arranged for their kids to be at sleepovers.

As soon as John stepped into the house, he smelled that familiar scent and was blown away. Ever since all their troubles had started, Jane had lost interest in cooking, entertaining, and all the other things, which she previously enjoyed – and such loss of interest can happen if one's struggling with depression.

John snuck up behind Jane – the exhaust fan was on so she didn't hear him come in – and threw his arms around her. Jane nearly jumped out of her skin. John noticed that her 'startle-response' had become really heightened in the last few months, almost as if she were more sensitive than usual. But seeing his face seemed to calm Jane down – she turned around, smiled, and then kissed John, like she really meant it.

The rest of the evening was full of surprises – great food and wine, and loads of laughter by their outdoor fireplace. It was just like old times.

John couldn't believe how far they'd come – if someone had told him six months ago that they could ever get there, he would've laughed at them … or cried at the situation of his own making.

Jane went upstairs, since John wanted to take care of the cleanup and dishes. When he entered their bedroom, half-expecting Jane to be asleep, she was waiting for him in bed, with telltale candles on the night tables. This was above and beyond anything that John could've hoped for.

John wrapped his arms around Jane and asked, "Are you sure?"

Jane said, "You have to ask? I planned the whole evening around it."

John was blown away and started to kiss Jane's neck, as he slowly undressed her out of her silky nightgown. Unfortunately, Jane's mind immediately raced to all the wrong places – imagining John with Lucy, wondering if Lucy's body was better than hers, or if Lucy was a better lover than her. Jane became stiff as a board – not what she'd expected after all that prep – anger had taken over her mind and body, for John having put her in that place, where she couldn't even enjoy making love to her husband.

From there, her mind raced to all the times when she'd tried hard to get John's attention – in much the same way – by putting herself out there sexually, when he was carrying on with Lucy. Again, not where she wanted or expected to go mentally.

John must've sensed her hesitation, since he knew her body as well as his own. He didn't want her that way.

But Jane insisted on keeping going, feeling that she had to cross that hurdle sooner or later.

Alas, while John's mind was more than willing, his body didn't cooperate – he lost his erection.

I've had many guys share that with me – be it fear of disappointing their partner, worrying about where her mind might go, or simply associating shame with sex; their equipment just won't work.

Of course Jane took that as a sign that he was either no longer attracted to her; or worse, "getting it elsewhere." She felt so vulnerable ... so exposed ... so ashamed. Talk about adding insult to injury!

Jane ran out of the room crying. When John followed her, she said, "Don't! I'm so humiliated! Bet this never happened with your whore!"

John didn't know *what* to say. He was crushed and just sat down on the floor against the wall; unable to move, as he heard the front door slam. He cried harder than he had ever before, but Jane had left the house to go for a drive, so she couldn't see his pain. And John was too broken to run after her.

When Jane returned hours later, she saw a suitcase on their bed – John was packing up some of his clothes to end their misery.

Jane didn't know whether to be angry or sad – but happy was definitely not an emotion in the running. Part of her wanted to stop him from leaving; part of her just wanted him to go – but that part feared that she'd be sending him right into Lucy's arms.

Jane remembered what I'd said, "While what he did was unacceptable, *he* isn't unacceptable. … There's a lot more to him than the hurt he caused! So don't put everything through that filter." Hearing that, she'd chimed in with, "In other words, hate the sin but not the sinner!"

So Jane mustered up her courage and said all that she could in the moment, "Where are you going to go? Why don't we sleep on it?"

John put the suitcase away, grabbed his pillow, and went downstairs to sleep on the couch.

It was the first time since the explosion that they'd slept apart – no matter how they felt, they'd agreed to sleep together; if for no reason other than to protect their kids from the truth.

It was the longest night of Jane's life – and possibly John's. She missed his warm body beside hers, the scent of his cologne when she cozied up to him and put her cold feet between his thighs, to warm them up.

The cold distance and the deadly silence wasn't something Jane could get used to – or wanted to get used to.

Jane would've given anything for them to be okay again – if she could rewind time, she'd whole-heartedly welcome his snoring as their biggest bedroom challenge.

So in the wee hours, as Jane saw the sun rise on the horizon, she went downstairs and invited John up to their bedroom, before the kids came home.

John gathered up the pile of crumpled up tear-soaked Kleenex on the floor that was a testament to *his* sleepless night and tossed it, before going upstairs with Jane.

The couch in the family room was directly beneath their marital bed in the master bedroom – they'd been just a few feet apart through the night, yet miles away in their pain. The only way to survive would be to support each other. Being angry and distant wasn't helping Jane any more than John – he was always triggered by the disengagement.

We all have to deal with the hurt and heal, whether we do it solo or together. Take it from me, together is half as painful, even when you feel anger at your partner for putting you there.

Jane decided to let her best friend back into her heart – she wasn't sure how she'd keep him there, but she was going to die trying!

Best way to address intimacy challenges is via healthy sexuality – the focus of our next chapter.

RECAP

- If it's a fight, sleep on it; if it's am outright war, don't make any rash decisions.

- If you're having physical symptoms in response to your emotions, defer your discussion to another time; but do schedule it in.

- Control your emotions vs allowing them to control you.

- Intimacy is the dance between the emotional and the physical, where trust provides the music to navigate the perfect moves.

When one stops using the excitement and intensity of sex to distract themselves from unpleasant feelings – only to learn that it just adds guilt and shame instead of helping – experiencing sex as a way to connect authentically, finally fills them and satisfies their unquenchable thirst. And when they experience that, anything short of it is just a reminder of the emptiness they felt before – even with affairs, because they're never fully authentic.

- Rebecca Rosenblat

Chapter 19

Intimacy & Healthy Sexuality

John and Jane came to see me for their next couple session. They wanted to discuss their way back into intimacy.

Jane shared how she couldn't un-see what she'd seen on John's computer – her active imagination had turned the script into a vivid movie that played in her head, over and over again, with the graphic details of a porno flick. ... And it wasn't just sex, because she'd read that he was thinking of his extra-curriculars while making love to her. How could she set that aside, hard as she tried?

So she asked me what every partner asks, "How do I know it will be different this time; that I'm not just being used for my accessibility when his mind is elsewhere?"

It isn't a question that I can answer definitively – I can only comment on the recovery process.

When one stops using the excitement and intensity of sex to distract themselves from unpleasant feelings – only to learn that it just adds guilt and shame instead of helping – experiencing sex as a way to connect authentically, finally fills them and satisfies their unquenchable thirst. And when they experience that, anything short of it is just a reminder of the emptiness they felt before – even with affairs, because they're never fully authentic.

This is especially the case with sex addiction. Once the addict experiences the difference between escape sex and real sex, they don't want to go back to the old way. For some, even the memory of that can take them to an anorexic phase, where they end up avoiding sex altogether, and may in fact be afraid of what it could do to them, and their recovery – which they don't want to compromise at any cost.

That said, in some cases, sexual anorexia can tie into the frustrated addict wanting to subconsciously punish an unsupportive partner, who's constantly shaming them and opening up their childhood wounds – making them feel helpless, and their recovery truly challenging. It creates the distance they need, and a sense of control over their sexuality, which had previously gone horribly out of their control.

I had a guy whose wife couldn't let the betrayal go, even after he'd recovered and they'd had intimate sex. She kept at him, and kept at him, disbelieving every word out of his mouth, for no good reason; even though she had nothing to contradict his stories – and believe me, she'd looked for it. Eventually, her anger started to take away from their sexual encounters. FYI, perpetual anger can stem from childhood experiences of abandonment and rejection.

In any case, the guy stopped having sex with her at that point, because he couldn't handle her anger. So she became more convinced than ever that he was getting it elsewhere.

Hearing that again and again, he felt defeated, stopped fighting for himself, and just shut down – what was the point, she wouldn't believe him anyway!

Then one day, when she accused him in session yet again, he covered his ears like a child, not wanting to hear her one more time, and blurted out, "This is bullshit! ... I'm done with disconnected sex, okay? I don't want it with *anyone*, least of all *you*! And when you're like this, that's exactly what it feels like ... far from the connection I crave. It's nothing more than a pity-fuck – I'd rather use my own hands – at least I'll get off at the mercy of someone who actually gives a shit, instead of just going through the motions to keep me around. ... Enough already! Just get off my back, okay? ... And if I'm so awful, let's end it, right here, right now, so we can both have some peace of mind and find real intimacy with someone else. I mean, why waste each other's time when this will never get any better? ... I'm done! That's it! Leave me alone!"

And with that, he marched out the door, as she muttered, "Good riddance" when I could see that that's not what she was feeling.

In the discussion that followed, I learned that it was all about control; controlling him, controlling the relationship, controlling her own vulnerability – the very thing that her husband so desperately craved, the thing that magical relationships are made of.

And that's where I wanted John and Jane to start – daring to be vulnerable, and doing their best to replace anger and hurt with love and mindful connection. I also wanted them to be aware of each other's needs, not just their own – be it to connect or withdraw – and accept them! For the latter, one needs to see the world through their partner's eyes.

To that end, I ask each party to begin their day by giving their partner three affirmations.

At the other end, I ask them to find some time in the evening, when they're not rushed, to have a quick, five-minute emotional check-in; where they ask about each other's day, how each party is feeling overall, and how they're feeling about the relationship. If anything major comes up, they're to set aside a time to discuss it, never during the check-in itself; otherwise they stop happening, when people are worried that they might not have time for an "all-nighter."

When I shared that with John and Jane, they nodded their heads, indicating they thought it was a good idea.

But then Jane asked another familiar question: how could ordinary intimacy with her possibly replace the lust-filled intensity John had experienced elsewhere? She just couldn't fathom that at all.

I love questions, because they allow me to put people's anxieties to rest. In this case, I responded by sharing the following story: Over a decade ago, I was asked to host a nightly, live, call-in, radio show for "Talk Radio for Guys." It was to be exciting, sensational, dramatic, sexy, and high intensity – all of which I achieved, along with more than was expected of me. In no time, it became the number one talk-radio show in Canada – in fact, we even gained a lot of the music listenership, which is unheard of. But as exciting and high intensity as it was – and everything leading up to it, as I planned for it throughout the day – I crashed after every single show, since I felt exhausted and let down, not to mention in violation of my core values, because it was really solicitous.

Then came 9/11 – a lot more intense than anything occupying the airwaves – leading the powers-that-be to cancel all programming, in favor of 24/7 talk of the world-altering event.

Shortly thereafter, I was approached by a lower key station, asking me to do a weekly, live, call-in show, every Friday night, about "intimate moments." The topics and calls weren't based in high intensity – in fact, it was quite the opposite. I mostly took calls from people who were looking to connect with someone, in their moment of need. Call after call, we made a connection – soon, we were getting calls from all over North America, and had an even bigger audience than before, albeit a low key one. Regardless, I left each show on top of the world, feeling giddy for having participated in something wonderful, basking in all the connections I'd made, which lasted throughout the rest of the weekend!

Having experienced both intense, meaningless sex as well as intimate sex, I can honestly say that the two shows gave me similar experiences to those. Had I not experienced that, I would've felt sex is sex (no matter what it looks/feels like) and a radio show is a radio show (no matter what it sounds like).

So to all those who've confused intensity with intimacy, I assure them that they're completely different entities – the former is exciting, dramatic, chaotic, depleting, and meaningless; the latter is warm, connected, peaceful, energizing and meaningful. Replacing the former with the latter may sound dull in theory, but when one tastes it, they agree how its lasting impact nurtures them and their authenticity, without any sense of shame or guilt. And whatever they're running from, loses its sting when they feel the love, support, and companionship of their partner, which nurtures them beyond the experience that was previously an end in itself!

Jane finally got it!

I went onto explain how one needn't choose between pleasure and connection, when they can have both. I shared the three types of sex that Dr. Sue Johnson – author of "Hold me Tight" identifies.

1.   <u>Sealed off sex</u>: It's just about getting off; so you need a bigger and bigger fix each time, with more and more novelty.

2.   <u>Solace sex</u>:   It's just about emotions, feeling desired/loved/etc. It makes one feel that if their partner's having sex with them, they must want them; but the flipside is, if they're not having sex with them, then something must be wrong – this is the place where a lot of partners end up.

3.   <u>Synchrony sex</u>:   This type of sex combines the first two; delivering both pleasure as well as connection. Dr. Johnson refers to it as "rocket sex".

No relationship can survive with just one or the other; you need both. In other words, no one is expecting you to do with less. In fact, it is my hope that you'll have more, so nothing short of it will ever do it for you again!

Now before we get into the nuances of connecting physically, I want to highlight what I call my "ten commandments" of healthy sexuality.

Ten Commandments of Healthy Sexuality

1. Take an electronic-free hour together every night, to listen to music, play a game/cards, plan romantic things, go for a walk, watch a sunset together, or indulge in romantic rituals. When you do watch TV together, hold hands, and try to chat during commercials.

2. Whenever you leave your home or return to it, hug each other for at least 20 seconds – full body, heart to heart, staring into each other's eyes. Kisses are wonderful as well, for forging that intimate connection. And since both hugs and kisses are an important part of nurturance, ask your partner for them when you need them; but tolerate your feelings if they aren't able to give them to you; and work through that together.

3. Tell your partner one thing you did to honor the relationship each day; and think of what it would be like to be your partner as you share.

4. Respect each other's authenticity without taking things personally – that includes respecting "yes" and "no" sexually, without feeling defeated. The idea is to listen without getting defensive, or reacting to your partner's point of view. And calm your anxieties in the face of your partner's upsets – don't use your discomfort as an excuse to avoid engaging sexually, or otherwise; or to create an entitlement for self-soothing elsewhere.

5. When you're with your partner, stay present and focus on staying connected. If something urgent is distracting you – like a deadline – let your partner know, so they don't perceive a lack of interest, or feel disconnected.

6. Discuss the purpose of the relationship from each party's perspective and see how you may be able to negotiate the differences. Beyond those differences, try to have some common goals and dreams.

7. Explore sexual potential by having deep conversations about what's possible. This should include what each of you wants and doesn't want – i.e. sexual limitations – within respectful boundaries, but with a willingness to meet each other's needs when possible. This is the only way to move past intercourse – which should never be the be-all-and-end-all. ... When you do pursue an idea, begin foreplay hours before you get to the bedroom, and be very deliberate with connecting and delighting in your partner.

8. Try to gaze into each other's eyes, at about a twelve-inch distance, for 4-6 minutes, at least once a week – it builds desire and connection at a neural level.

9. Teach each other what you like. Sit on the ground or a bed, facing each other, and take turns touching yourselves in ways you like to be touched, over your entire body, as a way of showing your partner in a non-threatening way; because suggestions must never feel like demands or put-downs. Besides, watching each other can be very erotic – something you should nurture anyways.

10. Take the time to experiment and communicate what it's like to move faster or slower; stronger or softer; be more focussed or diffused. Bring different touches into the bedroom, from how you use your hands to cook, garden, drive; to make your touch more deliberate and varied.

I could see that Jane and John were getting a bit over-whelmed, so I gave them very simple homework and sent them on their way. They were to take half an hour each evening, when they were most relaxed, and try out some of my suggestions, to start to get to know each others bodies and the touch that each party craves.

Sex wasn't supposed to be about intercourse or orgasm – just fooling around to see where it took them organically. But they *had* to schedule the time to connect! Spontaneity is highly over-rated, since in our busy world, things don't happen if you don't carve out time for them. So important things must never be left to chance. My definition of spontaneity is, scheduling some time to see where it takes you spontaneously!

John smiled at Jane and said, "Never thought I'd say that I'm actually looking forward to doing homework!" Not having the pressure to be erect on command, or perform on demand, made him feel more relaxed!

Wrong mindsets can truly tax healthy sexuality. Our next chapter will discuss how that can happen.

RECAP

- Never confuse intensity with intimacy.

- Sex and connection are like wine and cheese – better together than on their own.

- If you're sexually bored, chances are, so is your partner. Don't be afraid to discuss it.

- Intimacy takes a commitment – scheduling it in isn't a bad thing; neither is getting adventurous.

... I asked them to implement safe words, the easiest being traffic lights – green to reward any positive changes; amber to indicate that they were getting close to crossing the line on acceptable behaviour; and red to stop whatever was going on, no questions asked...

- Rebecca Rosenblat

Chapter 20

The Cost of Wrong Mindsets

Things started to go reasonably well for John and Jane, with the exception of Jane freaking out, every time John was in a bad mood. Her mind would race to worry about John going back to his old ways, when he'd snap for no reason; be on an emotional roller-coaster; or drive like a maniac.

I'd taught them to check in with each other, instead of jumping to conclusions. But Jane always feared that John's mood would get worse if she did.

I suggested that if there were no other causes for concern, she had to allow John his moods and not make them her own. She liked the idea. But it was still important for each of them to at least attempt to let the other know, when things felt like they were starting to unravel.

So I asked them to implement safe words, the easiest being traffic lights – green to reward any positive changes; amber to indicate that they were getting close to crossing the line on acceptable behaviour; and red to stop whatever was going on, no questions asked.

For example, if either one of them tried to stay connected when they would've previously checked out, the other could make a point of noticing it, by saying, "That was definitely a green moment."

Amber would be called if either party was starting to pull away or unravel, making the other party feel unsafe.

And if an argument was going out of hand, or John was starting to ignore Jane by paying attention to his electronics – or getting flirtatious at a party – she could say "red"; which would make John take notice of his behaviour and stop. Of course John was also allowed to use "red" if Jane was losing it for no good reason.

John and Jane got really creative with that. Once she was able to move past her sexual barriers, they used the light signals to amp up their sex life in healthy ways – both with respect to discussions, as well as trying out new things.

That said, at an emotional level, John did continue to struggle with shutting down, each time he felt insignificant to Jane.

And Jane continued to go from zero to sixty on her doubts in a nanosecond, if John did *anything* wrong.

I emphasized the importance of them being able to separate regular couple stuff from betrayal stuff; because making everything about that is a dangerous game that no one can win at – we don't live in a cocoon, so stressful things will happen; at work, for instance.

***

Jane's anxiety came to a pinnacle when she was asked to go away on an important business trip. It was a make it or break it move for her career, but she felt their relationship was more important. I asked her if she was worried about John's abandonment issues. She said, "No!" point blank.

Jane's concerns had to do with the fear of John cheating again, while she was away – he'd certainly have the opportunity. I reminded Jane that when John was cheating before, he was doing it while she was *in* town; sharing his bed. Point being: if someone really wants to cheat, they can *create* opportunities – they don't need their partner to be out of town; so there's no point in living with those kind of doubts.

John had worked really hard at showing Jane that that's not where his mind was at, so it was up to her to choose whether or not to believe him – no one else can make that decision for a partner!

Jane eventually decided to go away to represent her company at an international conference. She was really scared of doing the presentation, with her mind being elsewhere, but it went rather well. True to her character, Jane tried to call John right after, to share her success story with him. But John was nowhere to be found.

Jane's gut started to feel ill-at-ease, worrying that John and Lucy might have hooked up after all. So she called him numerous times, but to no avail. Eventually, his phone started going straight to voicemail. It could've been for any number of reasons, from running out of battery power to actually getting turned off. For Jane, there was only *one* reason: John was screwing Lucy and didn't want to be disturbed by the nuisance of her incessant calling.

Jane wanted to fly back home right away, instead of the following morning – damn the awards ceremony – to catch John in the act. She rushed to the airport and realized that the next flight home was sold-out.

Jane made a big enough stink at the ticket counter for everyone to notice. A woman walked up to her and said, "It sounds like you have an emergency – you can have my seat; I'll take the next flight out. I'm in no rush to get home." Jane couldn't believe her luck. She took the woman up on her offer, thanked her profusely, and boarded the plane.

Throughout the flight, Jane's bowels felt lose, and she even ended up making use of the barf bag. The flight attendants tried to make her comfortable, but to no avail. Jane ended up sharing a bit too much with one of them, who was quick to tell her that all men cheat if they can get away with it. Funny how this woman didn't know John from Adam, but she had a definitive opinion nonetheless. What's worse, Jane totally bought into it, whole-heartedly – as she always did, when someone was aligned with her doubts.

Whatever we focus on is all that we notice. Think about the last time you bought a car. While you were considering a particular brand and model, everywhere you looked, you saw that car. Since the brain can only process 2-3% of the information that comes its way, it misses everything else that it deems insignificant – Jane's mind was only able to focus on the one possibility that she was fixated on; unable to think of anything else.

Once she landed, Jane drove home like a maniac from the airport, to catch John, dodging what could've been a life-threatening accident.

When Jane arrived home, she found John's car in the driveway, but he was nowhere to be found. The house was completely silent – the kids were at sleepovers, since John had an early appointment and couldn't drive them to school. Jane started yelling obscenities.

Soon, there was a knock on the door. It was their neighbour, Nick. Jane didn't know whether to say "not now" and slam shut the door; invite him in to cry on his shoulder; or to drag him upstairs and have revenge sex with him ... right then ... right there – *why wouldn't she, since John was certainly having his way with Lucy*!

The knock became louder; more urgent. Jane yelled "coming" and swung open the door. Nick said, "I saw your car... thought you weren't expected home until tomorrow."

Jane said, "Yeah, that was the plan, but the bastard is at it again. I wanted to 'surprise' him."

Nick said, "You need to grab your purse and come with me. I have to drive you to the hospital."

Jane yelled, "What for?"

Nick shared, "John had a heart attack. He didn't want you to know, because he didn't want you to worry, or ruin your conference."

Jane's anger turned to terror. All she wanted to do now was set things right. She felt ashamed about all the ways that she'd cursed John, because she was *convinced* that he was up to no good.

In fact, she'd left him some horrible messages, which she hoped he hadn't retrieved. *What if something worse had happened, and that was the last thing he heard from her?*

Life truly is fragile. I worked with a couple – let's call then Lou and Emma. Just as Lou completed all his recovery work, was finally right with God and Emma, and ready to start the new phase in his life, he passed away quite unexpectedly.

175

I hugged Emma at his funeral, and said, "There's never a good time to go – this is just awful – but at least there was no unfinished business left between the two of you."

Emma responded, "That's exactly why I feel robbed. After decades, our marriage was finally on track."

At least her last words to him were loving, not accusatory!

Once you have the right mindset you can move forward, but not without forgiveness. The next chapter will focus on the importance of forgiveness, especially for the forgiver.

RECAP

- Respond, not react – the former has thought behind it, the latter does not.

- Words can never be taken back. So use the fast-forward technique to see if you'll eventually regret them; if so, then stop yourself before it's too late – no time like the present to take charge.

- It's important to invest time in recovery, but staying stuck without doing anything about it is a waste of time that'll never come back.

- When you must make a point, that has nothing to do with your primary issues, ask yourself if you want to be happy or right?

Chapter 21

Forgiveness vs Hostility

Jane asked Nick to drop her off at the emergency room entrance. She couldn't bear the thought of wasting the time it would take to go to the parking lot and walk back – it was ten minutes too many to be away from John.

Jane's belly was flip-flopping out of fear of John having heard her atrocious voicemails – how could she possibly face him after that? She felt truly ashamed and was beating herself up.

When Jane arrived at John's bed in the emergency room, and saw him hooked up to god-knows-what, she felt scared and remorseful. Even though she didn't want to wake him up, she gently took his hand and kissed it.

John opened up his eyes and smiled at her.

Jane said, "You didn't have to go through all this trouble to get me to cut my trip short – all you had to do was ask." But even as she teased him with that comment, Jane knew that wasn't the real reason she'd rushed back.

She was worried that he'd heard her voicemails and would see right through her comment. Jane hoped that wasn't the case and that her secret was safe with Nick – who'd supposedly called her against John's wishes, according to their cover story.

John squeezed her hand. Jane hoped that meant that he hadn't checked anything just yet – or perhaps he was just happy to be alive.

Once John was up to chatting again, he shared that he was truly surprised that he'd had a heart attack – and not exactly a mild one either. He was in pretty good shape, in his early forties, and he was trying to eat reasonably well. Jane wondered if stress had anything to do with it – he'd certainly been basking in it for months on end, without much of a break. But she was too scared to ask.

John insisted that Jane go home, because she'd had a really long day. But she didn't want to leave his side, so she made herself "comfortable" in the chair by his bed.

As Jane saw the sun rise in the window beside John's bed the next morning, she was grateful that they had the opportunity to usher in a new day together – a new life.

Once Jane had had a chance to speak with the doctor, who reassured her that John was going to be okay, she decided to go home, clean up, and pick up the kids from their sleepovers, to bring them into the loop. John had insisted that they not be told until Jane had returned from her trip.

When Jane arrived home, the very first thing she did was, look for John's phone. She couldn't find it anywhere.

Panic started to grip her throat so she could barely breathe, wondering if he had it with him all along, and had just turned it off in the hospital; meaning, he would've already heard her messages by now.

Jane decided to look one last place before giving up – John's car, since he was notorious for forgetting it in his cup-holder. Lo and behold, it was sitting there, lifeless.

Jane was relieved that it meant that more than likely, John hadn't checked his messages.

Since they'd offered each other total transparency, Jane plugged John's phone into the charger, clicked in his password, and tried to go through his voicemails.

John's mailbox was full with one nasty accusation after another, from Jane – she had no idea how vile she'd gotten. *Thank God John never heard any of those messages* – she wondered if that would've pushed him over the edge.

But Jane's relief soon turned into disgust – at herself. Had John not had a heart attack, she would've been convinced forever that something had gone on while she was away; when all he was guilty of was nothing more than leaving his phone in his car.

John would've eventually realized it when it was time to call her; but that unaccounted for period, where he had no alibi, could've ended their marriage, for no good reason.

Jane realized what an awful tragedy that would've been – one that would've destroyed them forever. It was time for her to do her own work, instead of being so focussed on John, relentlessly.

Before picking up the kids, Jane made herself a large coffee, and tried to rummage through the mess on her desk, to find the papers I'd given her; on what she needed to do to heal herself and the relationship – forgiveness being a case in point.

Jane found the papers buried beneath a pile of junk. More than likely, they would've been thrown out; or filed away without reading.

Thankfully, she recovered them and came across the following information:

Food for Thought for Partners

At some point in your healing journey, you need to begin to defog your own lens. What that means is, while there's no excuse for the wounding party's behaviors, you must quit focusing on them and start looking at your own behaviors, such as:

- making threats
- interrogating
- snooping
- engaging in verbal abuse
- shaming
- punishing
- numbing feelings with alcohol, compulsive over-eating, over-spending, overworking, engaging in other harming activities

Replacing such behaviors with the following can aid recovery in empowering ways:

- setting boundaries
- defining oneself (in terms of hopes, needs, desires, goals)
- committing to not compromising oneself
- getting self-worth from within

- focusing on self-care – HALT (if you're **H**ungry, you eat; if you're **A**ngry, you follow the anger to its source to learn what it's trying to tell you; if you're **L**onely, you call up someone reliable to connect with; if you're **T**ired, you get sleep)

It's about FORGING ahead. A great acronym for that suggested by IITAP is, F.O.R.G.E., which equals **F**orgiveness, **O**wnership, **R**estoration, **G**rowth, **E**mpowerment/Empathy. FYI, while most people can somehow manage most of that equation, they can become stuck in forgiveness, because they feel it minimizes their pain, gives the addict a get-out-of-jail-free card by letting them off the hook, etc.

So let's clarify what forgiveness is and what it isn't:

Forgiveness is:

- a gift of healing that you give to yourself, by giving up the resentment which consumes you

- a promise for a future that is built on more than hurts form the past

- a way to free up the emotional energy you need to create a new and exciting relationship – with yourself, your partner, or anyone else

- a gentle resolving of wounds that you've formerly refused to release

- giving up the need for sufficient punishment

- a key which allows you to unshackle yourself from the prison of painful memories – because the alternative is resentment, defined by Nelson

Mandela as the equivalent of taking poison and hoping it will kill the other person who hurt you.

Forgiveness is not:

- excusing your partner's deception or compulsive behaviors

- given only if asked for by the party that hurt you

- tolerating further betrayals

- allowing your partner to escape consequences of their choices

- looking the other way and pretending nothing's happening

- continuing to assume the victim role

- a way to guarantee that you'll be reconciled with your partner

- a way to change your partner's behavior

Ultimately, *you* have to make an active decision to move forward, and try to rebuild trust – no one else can do that for you.

If you're wondering, can you?   As the saying goes: *"Whether you think you can or you think you can't, you're right!"* - Anonymous

Our life begins with a need for reliability, so we can learn to trust. Our life matures when we learn to live with uncertainty. To live between those bookends makes our journey marvellously intriguing.

If all this sounds like clichés to you, let me leave you with this: There's an institution, which studies forgiveness. One of their most poignant studies with severely burned victims discovered that those who'd forgiven the person responsible for their burn – even when it was they themselves – healed much better and faster than those who did not.

Specifically, in case of skin grafting, most of the time, the very first graft took with those who could forgive; and those who couldn't forgive were still rejecting grafts at the fifth and the sixth try.

Whether we're looking at physical or emotional healing, the brain treats it in the same way.

So ask yourself, do you really want to suffer and compromise your healing because you can't forgive your partner – even when they disappoint you? I sincerely hope not! With forgiveness comes making amends – the focus of our next chapter.

RECAP

- Forgiveness is a gift you give yourself.

- Forgiveness is giving up the need for sufficient punishment.

- Living with uncertainty versus erroneous "certainty," is the only way of having a fair shot at saving your relationship.

- Holding on to a grudge is like taking poison and expecting the other party, who hurt you, to die.

Those who've caused the wounding have no idea what that looks like. In fact, they can become really upset with their partner if they're still holding on to the hurt, years later. In most cases they don't want to hold onto it – they'd rather crack up their skull and have amnesia to make it all go away. But hard as they try to conceal that wound and pray that they'll be completely done with it some day, it's always just beneath the surface and can rupture at any moment, given the right incentive through various triggers.

- Rebecca Rosenblat

Chapter 22

Making Amends

John came home to a really warm welcome, after being released from the hospital. Jane had gone above and beyond to make him comfortable – part gratitude for him still being alive, and part guilt for what she'd thought of him through his darkest moments.

John took a few weeks off, not just to recover physically, but also to complete the protocol for his sex addiction recovery and relapse prevention – his heart attack was a wakeup call, a reminder there's no time like the present.

John started seeing me again, every week. He'd let work get in the way and slacked off a bit, since he didn't think he needed therapy that badly any longer. The crisis was over and they seemed to be doing just fine, under the circumstances.

But Jane had felt anything but! Furthermore, for an addict to take that laze-faire attitude can be quite dangerous; it's foolish to assume that an addiction is under your control – by definition it's an addiction because it *isn't* under your control.

There comes a time in every couple's recovery when the partner starts to get really upset with the betrayer, when they stop working as hard as they did initially – it's the only reassurance they have, when trust isn't re-established just yet.

Besides, since the partner is still obsessing and quite often stuck, seeing their spouse "free" is really upsetting and scary for them. They assume that either they're back to cheating, or they no longer care, now that the crisis has passed.

Ironically, while the crisis may be done, the pain is anything but! Most wounding parties say that even when things go back to "normal", while their partner may be able to escape the pain every now and again, it sits in their gut non-stop – you can't escape from yourself! It's the worse kind of pain, since you feel responsible for the unbearable hurt you've caused someone you love, one that's changed who they are.

You witness it day in and day out – the life in their eyes is gone, along with their pep and swagger; they never look at you or the world the same way again; and they disengage during sex.

John had no idea that Jane was still feeling all that, even though she was very happy that he was alive, and they were still together. Being grateful for that and being able to forgive John helped quite a bit; but it didn't erase her wound.

Those who've caused the wounding have no idea what that looks like. In fact, they can become really upset with their partner if they're still holding on to the hurt, years later. In most cases they don't *want* to hold onto it – they'd rather crack up their skull and have amnesia to make it all go away. But hard as they try to conceal that wound and pray that they'll be completely done with it some day, it's always just beneath the surface and can rupture at any moment, given the right incentive through various triggers.

Thankfully, that's not the case most of the time, for partners who've invested in their own healing and recovery.

That said, there are some who stay stuck by choice, as a way of punishing their partner and ensuring that they never forget the damage their cheating caused. But those people are a minority – they often tend to view the world in black and white ways, hate to not be in-charge, enjoy the benefits of playing the victim (a passive-aggressive way of gaining control), can have a holier than thou attitude, and at times can be somewhat self-centered.

But Jane wasn't anything like that.

Jane just wanted to wake up one morning, feeling normal, where her biggest worry would be a work deadline, balancing the kids schedules with hers, or ensuring laundry was done on time and everyone had clean undies and socks – the very stuff that had irritated her in the past.

After watching John take his therapy and homework seriously, Jane started to catch glimpses of her old life coming back.

***

A few weeks after all kinds of healing, John got the green light to resume their sex life.

Jane was quite excited about that as well – she thought that having lost it yet again, he might view it through new eyes, as a valuable entity.

Jane agreed that it truly is the glue that binds the couple together, with the help of all those bonding hormones, like Oxytocin.

But they had to take it easy – it made for some amazing, languorous sex, where they deliberated over every single detail ... every touch ... every moment of exquisite pleasure.

Jane laughed and shared with me, "I guess every couple should go through an affair and a heart attack, to shake up things in the love and lust department".

I smiled and said, "Not the way I'd recommend you go about it. It's like the person who loses fifty-pounds due to an illness – not a diet I'd recommend either."

Jane said, "Touché" and went onto discuss the discomfort that she was having with some of her own feelings.

She shared that at times when images of John and Lucy fill her head during sex, she ends up changing the channel in her brain to one where *she's* the one who's with someone else – a new person who appreciates her and is really into her, instead of John going through the autopilot motions that felt like he wasn't into her at all; as if his mind had checked out and gone elsewhere.

I shared that while her fantasy is just her mind's way of protecting her and allowing her to stay in the moment; the stuff she was assuming about John was unfounded and dangerous – she needed to have an open and honest conversation with him; which is the whole point of recovery.

I also suggested that they be more open and honest about what they want in bed – it's secrets that got them into trouble in the first place.

Jane agreed and decided to have that conversation with John, now that he was "up" for more!

I suggested that she could download the "yes-no-maybe" list of sexual desires online, to get some ideas.

This list is a great way of sharing one's needs, without triggering the other party with unsettling doubts; via connecting those moves with other parties.

Once you make amends, you'll want to ensure you safeguard your relationship.

One of the ways of protecting your relationship is by identifying the triggers that unravel you and learning how to manage them. Find out how in the next chapter.

RECAP

- Owning your feelings and managing them is healthier than guessing at someone else's feelings and managing *them*.

- Opening up to each other, both in and out of bed, keeps your connection strong.

- Mind-reading can be dangerous – try to share what's on your mind, instead of allowing your partner to assume the worst.

- Life is fragile – don't waste good time after bad.

Drugs that are used to address erectile dysfunction – ED – are safe for healthy hearts, but men with cardiovascular disease should take special precautions; and some of them cannot use them under any circumstances. All arteries – not just those in the penis – are impacted by ED drugs, as well as organic nitrates, that are used to widen the arteries by increasing their supply of nitric oxide, in patients with angina (who have blocked arteries). So the two are not to be mixed; since they both act on nitric oxide, the combination can be serious, above and beyond a drop in blood pressure.

- Rebecca Rosenblat

Chapter 23

Unraveling Triggers

Jane shared some of the stuff that she'd found on the "yes-no-maybe sexual list" with John. They smiled at some of the suggestions in there that they'd never even thought of, that sounded like great ideas.

I was so excited to hear that they were finally able to have those open and honest conversations that they should've been having all along – the stuff that lovers discuss when they're trying to learn about each other.

With their sex life back on track, Jane's own sexual fears started to resurface. Having been the victim of sexual abuse, like many other victims who've been objectified, Jane had experienced a brief period – pre-John – where she'd used sex as her most valuable asset, to gain anything from validation to companionship.

She was scared that in allowing her mind to wander – so it doesn't get hijacked into the Lucy and John porno flick – some of her old memories might come back; not the abusive ones since we'd already worked through those, but technicolor scenarios with her *own* past lovers. Jane felt that would be like cheating.

I reminded Jane of the definition of cheating and said that only *she* would know where her head was at, and how it could impact her relationship with John.

Based on that, Jane felt that she might be headed into dangerous territory, so I suggested that she try to focus on sensations and deep breathing, to shift gears on her theater of the mind.

The other thing that Jane started doing was reading risqué romance novels, like *50 Shades*, so her imagination wouldn't wander off to real people; just interesting new scenarios where she imagined John *really* being into her.

It seemed to do the trick, because things started to heat up between them, as John's stamina improved.

Then one day, as Jane was cleaning the bathroom, she went into John's drawer where he kept his vanity items, and found a vial of Viagra. Jane was horrified at the very thought – the secrecy was even more upsetting to her, because she couldn't fathom a good enough reason for it. Jane wondered if it was there for her or someone else? She didn't know what was worse – him using it to boost himself for double-dipping, or him being unable to get it up with her, without the help of a little blue pill. ... See what I mean about triggers?

Triggers always seemed to hijack Jane's brain to the worst-case scenario; and John had to experience her wrath as a result – not for something he did in the moment, but something she imagined. It was really frustrating for him, because when she went there, there was no talking to her; so he'd check out rather than getting into it with her. He figured that she'd be upset either way; but if he didn't say anything, at least he wouldn't say the wrong thing – not the ideal solution by any means, but that's where he went.

Jane was starting to get that. Furthermore, having been instructed to put her brain in gear before opening up her mouth, unfiltered, she decided to come to me to discuss the issue first, before unraveling with John. And I was really glad for it. There were so many options besides the two that she was hung up on; for instance, John was the right age for erectile challenges; not to mention the possibility of cardiovascular issues – the latter scared me a bit, because those drugs are often contraindicated for most heart conditions. Another possibility: John had been under a lot of stress, which releases cortisol – the stress hormone – and that in turn constricts blood vessels, so a man doesn't get the full blood flow to the penis that's necessary for an erection.

I was really glad that Jane had shared that information with me – beyond addressing her fears, I wanted to ensure that John's doctor was in the loop about him taking Viagra, for obvious reasons. So I asked Jane to check if the vial had a doctor's name on it, so I could make sure that the drug was properly prescribed and being monitored, versus something he'd bought online; which is never a good idea, for many reasons, not the least of which is that they can be cut with harmful substances. The reason certain drugs require a prescription is because they need to monitored carefully.

I was hoping that John had obtained the drugs via the right channels, and that his cardiologist had greenlighted them.

As a sidebar, I'd be remiss if I didn't point out the following, since I know too many men who take those pills to counter-act performance anxiety, after infidelity has rocked their relationship:

Drugs that are used to address erectile dysfunction – ED – are safe for healthy hearts, but men with cardiovascular disease should take special precautions; and some of them cannot use them under any circumstances. All arteries – not just those in the penis – are impacted by ED drugs, as well as organic nitrates, that are used to widen the arteries by increasing their supply of nitric oxide, in patients with angina (who have blocked arteries). So the two are not to be mixed; since they both act on nitric oxide, the combination can be serious, above and beyond a drop in blood pressure.

In any case, Jane reached into her purse for the pills – she'd brought them to show them to me; as if I needed proof. Since the cheating party gets accused a lot, they start to challenge accusations, so the wounded party always feels that they have to prove things – not that it stops them when they can't.

While Jane was handing over the pills to me, she saw the date and the doctor's name – their family doctor had prescribed them nearly a year ago, when John was indeed double-dipping! Jane was furious that he still had them. I suggested that he could've forgotten about them, because taking those pills with his heart condition was highly unlikely.

Jane decided to count them and slip them back into John's bathroom drawer. She was planning on counting them daily, to see if anything went missing; and whether or not it coincided with them making love.

I suggested that Jane try having an open and honest conversation with John; but her need to play detective took over and she insisted that she had to test John, hoping with all her heart that her fears were unfounded.

I reminded Jane that I wasn't going to collude with her by keeping any secrets on her behalf. Meaning, while I wasn't going to call up John and tell him what she was up to, I was going to ask Jane to bring up her concerns in the next couple session, booked for two weeks down the road.

Jane was going to make the most of the opportunity, and promised me that she'd drop it by then, and be willing to discuss it when I brought it up.

I'd hoped with all my heart that it was an old vial that John had forgotten about, for myriad reasons.

Whether or not, Jane was treating it as a current betrayal, she felt that John had had many opportunities to come clean, especially when they'd laid out everything on the table, so she couldn't understand why he'd kept that from her.

When I suggested embarrassment as a possible reason, Jane wasn't having any of it, since what John had already shared was significantly more embarrassing – she did have a point!

And that's essentially what happens – even past indiscretions start to feel current, when the secrecy is in the present moment. It's the "You're still lying to me" sentiment; and its close cousin, "So what else have you been keeping from me?".

***

Two weeks later, Jane took the lead in putting it out there at the very beginning of our couple session; before I could bring it up. She said, "John took a Viagra the last time we made love, without telling me" – point blank.

John looked shocked, and asked, "How did you know that?"

Jane said, "Is that all you have to say? ... You seem more concerned about getting busted than taking it and lying to me about it. I thought we said, no more secrets."

John apologized and Jane went onto asking him, "Are you sorry that you need pills to be able to get it up for me, or sorry that you got caught?"

I intervened with, "John, have you run this by your doctor?" John shook his head to indicate that he hadn't.

I followed up with, "Well you *really* need to do that. In the meantime, maybe you can explain what's going on?"

John confessed that every time him and Jane tried to make love, he lost his erection due to performance anxiety.

He had no problem becoming erect, when he just saw Jane stepping out of the shower; but the fear of what must be going on in her head while making love, made it very challenging for him to measure up.

Jane scowled, "Don't you worry, I have amazing things going on in my head – none of which have anything to do with you!"

John looked defeated and shook his head. After the longest three seconds of silence, he finally managed a barely audible "What's *that* supposed to mean?"

Jane hissed, "So *now* he's worried about what I'm thinking! Did you think of me when you were with her ... even once?"

I felt I was losing control of the session, as Jane started to race backwards in her fit of anger. I asked her, "What are you hoping to do here? Please help me understand it."

Jane said, "I'm not sure. I guess I'm just pissed that he's still keeping things from me ... and part of me is wondering if he took them way back when, to keep up with the double-dipping?"

I asked Jane to get to the heart of her fears, and directly ask John to address those.

But she marched out, since she wasn't going to believe anything that he had to say at that point anyway.

John ran out after her – I was so proud of him. Most guys figure that a woman must need her space when she runs out, just like they themselves would; and they're happy that they somehow dodged the bullet.

But Guys, take it from me, nine out of ten women always want you to run after them, even when they try to resist.

John had finally figured that out, and caught Jane just on the other side of the door; where he took her in his arms and said, "I'm so sorry I've hurt you *so* deeply that you can't even hear me out."

Validation – another big thing that partners crave – you can never have enough of it!

That said, while validation is critical, creating drama isn't the way to solicit it; even when your partner only hears you when you amp things up.

In the next chapter, we'll discuss giving up the false need for drama.

RECAP

- Don't ask a question if you're not interested in hearing the answer – or believing it.

- Don't assume the worst if your partner is struggling with erectile challenges. The stress hormone – cortisol – causes a constriction of blood vessels and a drop in testosterone; both of which cause sexual issues.

- If you pay more attention to your past versus your present or the future, it's like driving a car by looking in the rear-view mirror – you're bound to crash.

- Validation of feelings doesn't mean you agree on the subject matter. It's just an empowering way to connect – so why fight it?

Chapter 24

Giving Up the Drama

John was furious with Jane. *When was her constant state of suspicion going to end? Was it ever going to end?*

At first, John had accepted it, because of what he'd done to her – she was never a suspicious person prior to what had transpired. He'd also felt that he'd done this bad thing so he was to make up for it forever.

Furthermore, John respected the fact that I'd said that if Jane had a legitimate question, he was to answer it; provided that she was willing to at least *consider* that he was telling the truth. But this was neither a question, nor a willingness to hear his honest answer; so John was livid.

John said, "Maybe it's time to cut our losses and separate". Having had the heart attack was a sobering experience for him; one, which taught him that life is finite – so he wasn't willing to waste his or Jane's life on constantly tiptoeing through a minefield. He felt they both deserved to be loved whole-heartedly, where neither side would have to hold anything back. He couldn't change the past, but he felt that he'd worked hard to change the present and the future, but it hadn't been acknowledged in any way whatsoever. The only feedback that Jane gave him was when he screwed up – or when she *thought* that he'd screwed up.

John asked me for a therapeutic separation agreement, so they could take some time apart and sample what life would be like without each other; and then decide once and for all whether or not they were willing to put all this behind them.

A therapeutic separation contract clarifies that the separation is about getting to a healthy place, not dating others to see what else is out there. And all domestic and financial details are clarified ahead of time.

I suggested that we take that up in our next couple session, along with putting the Viagra story to rest, since it was the straw that finally broke John's back.

Basically, John had purchased it to use with Lucy when they were having an affair, since sex with her was full of anxiety and guilt and not nearly as good as it was with Jane – something that a lot of people share with me; since their spouse knows their body like no other, and the connection is more intimate. In some ways, that's the whole point – i.e. avoiding intimate contact.

In any case, since the pills had nothing to do with him and Jane, he'd left it out of the disclosure, as one of those irrelevant details which didn't belong in there.

Then recently, since John already had the pills, he used them to fight performance anxiety – without thinking. He didn't want Jane to fear that it was a result of her not doing it for him – a place that too many partners go, far too often, including Jane.

I hoped with all my heart and soul that John and Jane could come to an agreement, so as not to compromise all the hard work that they'd invested in thus far.

Typically, if the cheating party has any hope that their partner is doing their best to move forward and will eventually get there one day, they do whatever it takes to make that happen. But if they feel that their partner is completely stuck in the "unfairness" aspect, is unable to move past it, and/or will keep them in check by constantly reprimanding them into behaving, they lose hope and may want to cut their partner loose to find someone else who'll make them happy – and of course do the same for themselves. When that happens, the fear of losing their spouse can act as a rock bottom moment for the *partner*, making them decide to do their own work, instead of stalling their journey as a couple; or worse, ending the journey altogether.

In other cases, the cheating party may become belligerent, with a sense of righteous indignation, because they know they're not doing anything wrong any longer, but the partner simply can't let go. In the event that that happens, it's critical to keep in mind that the partner has no way of reading their mind, so that attitude can be truly disruptive.

That said, sometimes being stuck has to do with the wounded party assuming a victim status, which doesn't help anyone, least of all them – it makes them feel like everything is out of their control. Knee-jerk victimhood is a coping mechanism that's most common with – but not limited to – the youngest child in the family, who can automatically whine or cry at the slightest provocation.

When a betrayal has taken place, the person playing the victim can easily turn into a persecutor and vise versa; so I have couples do an exercise which demonstrates just that – The Karpman Drama Triangle – which can be quite transforming for many.

The Karpman Drama Triangle

The Drama Triangle is a social model of human interaction, which maps out a type of destructive interaction that can occur between people in conflict. It was conceived by Dr. Stephen Karpman, M.D., who used triangles to map conflicted or drama-intense relationship transactions.

In this particular triangle, he defined three roles in the conflict; Persecutor, Rescuer (the one up position) and Victim (one down position). The Victim in this model is not intended to represent an actual victim, but rather someone feeling or acting like a victim.

The Victim's stance is "Poor me!" because they feel victimized, oppressed, helpless, hopeless, powerless, unable to make decisions, and so on. Throw some alcohol in the mix and they can take it to new heights.

The Rescuer's line is "Let me help you." A classic enabler, he/she feels guilty if he/she doesn't try to rescue.

However, the rescuing has negative effects: it keeps the Victim dependent and gives them the permission to fail. The Rescuer does this because if they focus their energy on someone else, they can ignore their own anxiety and issues.

The Persecutor insists, "It's all your fault." The Persecutor is controlling, blaming, critical, oppressive, angry, authoritative, rigid, and superior.

In general, participants tend to have a primary or habitual role (victim, rescuer, persecutor) when they enter into the drama triangle. Participants first learn their habitual role in their family of origin.

That said, even though each of them has a role that they primarily identify with, once in the triangle, participants rotate through all the positions, going around the triangle, again and again.

For example, the wounded party may play the victim role and get really upset with the cheating party. As they yell at them, blame them, slight them, take away their voice, they turn into the persecutor and the cheater turns into the victim. After enough accusations, the cheater will fight back, and the dynamic switches again. Or, either party may try to end the situation with a rescue attempt, which never works, since the focus always ends up being on the other party. Bottom line, no one ever wins when they enter the drama triangle. The idea is to get out of the triangle, as soon as you recognize it.

I generally pull out three chairs with the three titles taped on them. I ask each party – in the couple-ship – to sit in the chair they most identify with.

Then, I ask the person in the victim chair to start sharing what they're feeling. While they do that, they realize that they've turned into the persecutor, so they switch chairs and sit in the persecutor's chair, and the party being accused takes the victim's chair.

Once they've had enough, they start to blame the wounded party, for all the wrongs they've done to hurt them, for not taking any responsibility, and for wanting to stay stuck.

The couple ends up switching chairs again, because the victim has now become the persecutor, and vise versa. I'm sure you get the picture.

It's a great tool to mobilize people, particularly the party that's playing the victim!

At this point in their journey, both John and Jane had mentally sat in the proverbial victim seat; as well as the persecutor seat.

So we started the next couple session with the drama triangle. John saw where I was going with that.

I asked Jane to share what it would take to stop running in the triangle, to protect herself from getting hurt again.

Tears welled up in her eyes, as she said, "I think John's pretty much doing what I need from him, already. It's *I* who's stuck and needs to do the work to move forward. Never realized how I persecute him, while still managing to feel like the victim!"

I asked Jane if there were benefits to her being stuck – half expecting that she'd attack me. This time, she didn't; and just said, "I suppose it's been my way of protecting myself. I've been afraid that if my pain gets forgotten, it would be too easy for John to hurt me again. ... This is my way of controlling the situation. ... Letting it go because of our work together felt like we'd be tying up lose ends with a tiny little bow, and setting everything aside like a clean little package, that'll get placed on a shelf somewhere – like it never mattered – and John would just get away with everything."

Pulling out the separation agreement now would've hurt Jane deeply – not what John ever intended. So he never brought it up, and just asked me to help them with some tools to stop their flight down the slippery slope where Jane's worries push him down oh-so-easily, and his pain gains momentum faster than anything that he could possibly keep up with.

After putting drama behind you, you'll be able to see clearly and become unstuck – the next chapter.

RECAP

- Assuming the victim status gives up control over a given situation.

- Every "victim" ends up becoming a persecutor at some point, when they start to attack the other party. Recognizing that and giving up both roles is the only way of stepping out of the drama triangle – you never win if you stay in it, solo or as a couple.

- If you're stuck in a given situation, ask yourself what benefits you might be reaping, and what will it take to become unstuck – if you don't know, how can you expect your partner to know, and make things right.

- People who grow up in drama often seek it out – albeit subconsciously – because it makes them feel that everything is normal/familiar. If they don't see drama, they can become worried that something's wrong, or the passion is gone, so they may end up creating it; at times for no good reason.

... a lot of these people can only see the world through their own lens – they have a really hard time seeing it through other people's eyes, particularly their partner's. So much so, that even when their partner is expressing a hurt, they slip into "but what about me" mode. And when they go to their own therapist, they often waste the session expressing their grievances, versus going deeper, where they can heal...

- Rebecca Rosenblat

Chapter 25

Becoming Unstuck

It's always a really exciting day for me when the light that had left a partner's eyes returns. Since couples come to see me after the light's already gone, for me, it's like seeing a new person for the very first time.

When Jane walked through my door for our next session, I saw that all-too-familiar light – a telltale sign if you may – which speaks volumes to announce the transition into becoming unstuck.

Before we go any further, I want to comment on some of the commonalities I witness with people who tend to stay stuck the longest.

Most of them come from rigid households where the world was seen as right and wrong; where they were expected to uphold more than their fair share of responsibility; where they had to live up to high expectations and a certain level of perfectionism – the latter is so strong in fact, that if they're asked to wear a shirt inside out to work for a day, just to prove that they don't have to be perfect, most of them can't do it!

What's more, those impossible standards can make them act judgemental, thereby appearing quite offensive – even to friends and acquaintances.

And it doesn't end there either. They have a tendency to get stuck in the "why's" of every situation, even though they have no intention of listening to anyone's answers; just rebutting.

Now I'm not suggesting that other partners don't want to know why something happened; just that these partners can become paralysed by it – and no matter what explanation is offered them, they dispute it, if it doesn't resonate with their own view of the situation.

I've had many partners tell me point blank "I'm not buying it" no matter how much evidence I can offer otherwise.

Beyond that, a lot of these people can only see the world through their own lens – they have a really hard time seeing it through other people's eyes, particularly their partner's. So much so, that even when their partner is expressing a hurt, they slip into "but what about me" mode.

And when they go to their own therapist, they can often waste the session expressing their grievances, versus going deeper, where they can heal.

As such, their partners complain that they come home from their sessions more upset than before – which can happen regardless, since it isn't easy to go into those tough places.

At the end of the day, the therapist is like a doctor who pokes and prods to find the area that hurts the most; and then they go after it, because they feel that's where the problem lies.

Emotional work is no different.

Jane had expressed her fair share of those symptoms, right down to getting furious when I poked too hard, or forced her to see things through John's eyes.

But this session was quite different, because she started off by admitting to her bird's eye view of the whole situation. She went so far as to say that while she'd appreciated John for what he brought to her life, she couldn't appreciate his suffering, which was constant, since he couldn't forgive himself.

John had voiced that he wished that Jane would do something equally awful, so they could be even; painful as that would be. He'd felt that he could tolerate his own pain significantly better than hers. In the moment, her pain had become his, so he was carrying both!

Had John known that Jane was fostering her own infidelity – albeit a fiscal one, with loads of retail therapy – he might've felt a bit "better."

Then again, Jane was going to make the obvious comparison – i.e., that it was nothing compared to *his* brand of infidelity. It's a place where quite a few partners end up; though some go there to make themselves look more attractive, so their partner desires them more, even though that's not what any of it is about – some actually find their partners to be more attractive than those they've cheated with. Think of all the celebrities with gorgeous partners, complete with fame and fortune, who were caught cheating with people who weren't even in the same ball park!

I asked Jane how she could compartmentalize her own wrong-doings and childhood hurts which resonated with his, instead of laying everything out on the table as she'd insisted that he do.

Jane joked that her brain was like a waffle. And the funny thing with her and waffles was, when she did have one for real, she managed to put a dollop of syrup into each and every compartment, separately, instead of just slathering it on the whole dang thing like most people do. John had shared in another context – when he was calling her anal – that she'd always say that she was just making sure she gets every corner, instead of admitting to being that anal!

Jane went onto to confess that her waffle brain was what allowed her to cope with her childhood. Had she not separated everything into different compartments, she wouldn't have been able to function – certainly not at the standard that was expected of her.

Even through her short promiscuous phase, the way Jane managed was by separating those activities from her wholesome living and church activities; convincing herself that one had nothing to do with the other.

But the reality of the situation may have been that she was using that space to silently rebel, or feel some power over a territory that no one else could control – one where she could be the "bad girl" versus the one who judged them. She was able to separate the two almost like those who go to bawdy houses to indulge their dark shadows, through fetishistic games.

The more we discussed Jane's childhood, the more she realized that she had punished John for something that she herself had done – creating a little compartment to flee from impossible standards.

But John let her get away with it, because he was focused on making her happy.

I've had many men confess that they spent their entire marriages trying to uphold the adage "happy wife, happy life," to the point of neglecting their own needs.

But since no one can ever be responsible for their partner's happiness, it's a setup for failure; one that makes them horribly miserable and unhappy.

Ultimately, these guys have a high need for external validation for their efforts.

And when it isn't forthcoming, it can lead to dark moods, angry outbursts, and seething resentment; which in turn can cause a sense of entitlement, that leads them to places which *can* and *do* cause unhappiness for the both of them. What they need to do is, be responsible for their *own* happiness; because when they're unhappy, they make their wives the unhappiest of all – the very thing they work so hard to avoid at all costs.

At the end of the day, it's about knowing what you want, and what your partner needs, by paying attention; and expressing both in a way that's well received – i.e. knowing each other's love and sex languages (more on that later). Some men are baffled when their wives ask them for a divorce, when they'd been expressing their frustrations all along – they just weren't listening.

But as far as happiness goes, I always told men that I dated that they weren't responsible for my happiness – I choose to make myself happy in every possible way – but if they dared to do something to make me unhappy, then we'd have a serious problem; and they'd have to own that one for sure.

When I shared that with Jane, she saw the simplicity in that statement.

She smiled and said: "I guess unhappiness can also be a choice to some extent; as I've clearly been choosing that subconsciously, instead of happiness – not that I enjoyed it, but the sentiment somehow suited the situation."

I retorted, "But as you can see, you can *change* the situation – and if I'm right, it appears like you're ready to do that now."

Jane said, "I am, but I have one last question, before I take that step. ... Can you please give me one of your analogies that'll reaffirm that after all the work we've done, John isn't just going to turn around and return to his old ways?"

I get that question a lot, so I was able to pull out the requested analogy out of my back pocket, just waiting to jump out. I shared the following with Jane:

Imagine that John was 600 pounds. One day, he decided to lose 400 pounds, for his own sake, and because he could see that you couldn't stand to look at him any longer. So he worked really hard to get to that place. Once John reached his goal, he started to feel really good about himself, having shed all that excess baggage. He felt healthier; he loved the way you looked at him; and life felt great in general. Naturally, John wanted to stay there forever. Now if John were to gain a few pounds, unlike the rest of us who might be a bit annoyed, he'll more than likely hit a place of panic, since he'll seriously worry about ending up right back where he started. He knows what that looks like, so his fear will be significantly worse than anyone else who hasn't been there, and experienced firsthand how awful that can feel – a place one would never want to return to, after all the hard work they'd put into getting away from it; the kind of work that'll feel daunting if it had to be repeated.

Jane smiled and leaned forward in her seat, like she had something up her sleeve.

Our time was almost up, but Jane asked if she could invite John in for the last few minutes.

I didn't even know that he was in the waiting room, but I was happy to oblige, since she was beaming with the excitement of whatever she'd planned.

John came in and sat down. Looking at the confused expression on his face, it was obvious that like me, he too didn't have a clue what Jane was planning.

Jane reached into her purse and pulled out a hammer – both John and I were taken aback.

She rested the hammer on my coffee table, making me a bit antsy around what she was about to do. I remembered her and John sharing that she turned into a "bat shit crazy banshee" at her worst moments.

But then, just as I was wondering if I had to call security, she pulled out a waffle that was packed in saran wrap, and placed it on the table.

She then asked John to hold the hammer with her – almost like a cake knife to cut a wedding cake together, like a bride and groom – and gently flattened the waffle, while announcing that she was done with compartmentalizing her life, and was going to turn a new leaf with John, with no more walls.

John teared up and hugged her tightly, almost like he was going to crush her bones. I wondered if I'd have to call security after all, because of the force of his hug – sorry, I digress!

Becoming unstuck opens up the doors to starting to enjoy each other once again.

In the next chapter, we'll tackle love and sex languages, so you can do that in a way that your partner can comprehend and appreciate.

RECAP

- Being judgemental never accomplishes anything – it can only create a rift.

- The more someone invests in their recovery, the farther they get, the less likely they are to undo what they worked so hard to accomplish.

- No one is responsible for your happiness, only *you* can make yourself happy; but others can certainly make you unhappy – it's important to know the difference!

- If your partner gets easily triggered or becomes hypervigilant, it could be because their reality took them to places they never thought possible, which can make anyone paranoid. It's much like a person who battled cancer but is now in remission – any future lumps or hint of similar symptoms will terrify them, while the average cancer-free person would be far less frightened.

Chapter 26

Love & Sex Languages

Now before I get back to John and Jane – don't you just hate the suspended animation – I have a story to share with you. Stay with me – it'll connect to them eventually.

A couple came into my office not that long ago. I asked them, what brought them in. The wife (let's call her Rachel) responded that it was because the husband (let's call him Daniel), didn't love her.

Daniel blew out a frustrated breath and said, "Why the hell do you think that? I wake up at 5am, after having worked until 11 pm the night before, to shovel the snow, scape the ice off your car windows, make sure you have enough gas in the tank, and warm up your car so you don't have to. ... If *that* aint love, what is?"

Rachel said, "That's really sweet, but you never *tell* me that you love me."

Daniel responded, "And you keep telling me that you love me, but how about *showing* me for a change? Actions speak louder than words."

I could tell they both loved each other but weren't feeling it. My guess was that they probably had different "love languages." Dr. Gary Chapman, author of "The Five Love Languages" identifies five different languages in which we give and receive love.

The reason he calls them languages is, because unless you express love in someone's love language, they don't get it. Here's what that looks like:

1. Acts of service: These people show love by doing nice things for those they love; and they only feel loved when someone does nice things for them – think Daniel.

2. Words of affirmation: These people show and receive love by saying and hearing the right words, including, "I love you!" – think Rachel.

3. Touch: These people love hugs, kisses, cuddling, and yes intimacy – both giving and receiving – it isn't just about sex.

4. Quality time: These people give and perceive love by having quality time together. If you don't make time for them, they can feel unloved.

5. Gifts: These people love to give and receive gifts.

Can you see what happened with Daniel and Rachel? They just weren't expressing love in a language that their partner could comprehend.

With another couple, he bought her jewelry for her birthday and took her out for dinner; she made him his favorite meal for his.

Both parties were really upset, because her language was acts of service; his, gifts. So neither one of them felt loved or that a fuss was made over them on their birthdays.

The problem was, each party showed love to the other in the way that *they* felt loved, not the way their *partner* did, thereby missing each other.

So what does this have to do with John and Jane? We were about to find out. Having seen John and Jane continue to doubt each other's love, even after recovery and healing had taken place, made me wonder if they were victims of the same confusion as the above couples – along with at least a dozen others that I'd seen just in the last month.

So I asked them to take Dr. Gary Chapman's love languages test online, to see if they spoke the same or different languages.

I urge all of you to do the same – it can be one of the biggest eye openers, especially if you're not feeling loved.

As it turned out, Jane's love language was quality time; which is why she felt unloved when John was pulling away, and tried to make it right by arranging for things that they could do together. John's love language was words of affirmation – so when Jane disapproved, he didn't just feel shame; he felt unloved. It was also the language that he used to show Jane his love, by carefully picking his words to reach her heart and soul.

I shared with John and Jane that when people speak different love languages, it's critical to learn how to love each person in *their* language, not your own. Dr. Chapman's book does a remarkable job showing you how to learn and negotiate different love languages – a must read!

Speaking of languages, Dr. Doug Weiss – yes, the same Weiss-man from before – has identified five sex languages, in his book by the same title: "5 Sex Languages". Finding out your partner's sex language, and incorporating it into intimacy can take sex off the charts – another must read!

So what exactly are those five sex languages?

1. <u>Fun</u>: These people hate planned sex, because they'd rather be spontaneous – different places, positions, experimenting with different things, creatively exploring all elements – as long as it's fun. As such, they can take risks, and push the right buttons to get their partner to do the same.

2. <u>Desire</u>: These people want to be desired, craved, wanted, pursued, every which way – sexy texts through the day, playful voicemails, intentional come-ons – because affirmation is important to them. They don't do rejection very well, so don't tease them if you don't mean it.

3. <u>Pleasure</u>: These people will pursue pleasure to the nth degree, chasing new ideas, getting creative, exploring different ways of giving and receiving pleasure, to expand their sexual repertoire. When they make love, they're all in.

4. <u>Patience</u>: These people place a high value on finding a safe, secure place, with loads of time – so don't rush them. They take their time, teasing with the lightest touch, but lots of it. They're not into anything rough, or being spoken to harshly, because gentleness is their middle name. After orgasm, they like to lay around, cuddling, spooning, lightly touching, chatting in a meaningful way – "pump and dump" is highly unacceptable to them. If you're not into slowly taking your time, laying around, this person is not for you!

5. <u>Acceptance/Celebration</u>: For these people, the pleasure of sexuality is holistic. They make love with their heart, and desire all of you to make love to all of them. They need a high level of acceptance and intimacy, even in non-sexual parts of their relationships. Sex starts long before the clothes come off, because they have to get everything right. They tend to be givers, and love to be valued for mind, body, and soul, in a meaningful way.

When I talked about the sex languages with John and Jane, she started to chuckle. "Oh that's why? ... I always wondered why John always needed to be desired – if he didn't feel it, he'd pout like a chick."

She then winked at him and said, "I think I'm a pleasure slut – patience was never my virtue, not in bed anyways."

John laughed, "Whatever happened to quality time?"

Jane smiled, "Sexy time *is* quality time!"

John reached over and ran his fingers through Jane's hair. The simple gesture looked so natural, with not a comma of hesitation on her part, or a smidgen of tentativeness on his.

I walked over to my bookcase and pulled out a copy of *"5 Sex Languages"* so Jane could snap a picture of the cover with her iPhone.

I'd hoped that speaking in Jane's sex language would make John a cunning-linguist in bed!

The book wasn't a hard sell by any means. The couple's grins spoke volumes!

The final thing that I wanted them to do was, attend my Hold Me Tight intensive, designed by the number one marital therapist in the world, Dr. Sue Johnson; based on her book by the same title, and all her research and training in Emotionally Focused Therapy.

Sue's work is another game changer, since it reveals the map to loving in a way that really works – it isn't a mystery, as we've been led to believe.

Ultimately, we want to know that our beloved is there for us, they have our back, they'll come when we call, and we matter to them!

Couples who attend learn how they evaluate their relationship through those four questions.

Beyond that, they also learn to identify and articulate their needs; stop the negative dances that we all get caught up in; identify their raw spots; forgive injuries; and forge ahead with a long, loving, lasting relationship.

What I was trying to do with John and Jane was, shift gears from months of recovery work on to growth and building work.

I believe that if you don't usher a couple into that next stage, the emphasis of their relationship work remains betrayal-focused, when they're about so much more than that.

John and Jane were really excited by everything they'd learned, and the tools I gave them to move forward.

All they had to do to stay on track was to complete my Needs Inventory (see Appendix) and share it with each other.

John and Jane acknowledged that it was important to stay on the right track, and never lose their way again.

But they wanted to ensure that they were on the right journey first and foremost – so they said that they were going to change the agenda for our next session.

Loving the right way leads to new beginnings and happy endings.

I love happy endings, don't you? If so, read the next chapter to make yours happen!

RECAP

- Know each other's love and sex languages to love and pleasure in a way that's well-received.

- If you have each other's back, matter to each other, and are there for each other, all else will fall into place.

- Focus on what's important for the relationship, not either party, so you'll always stay on the same side, without any resentment!

- If you fill up each others emotional bank accounts, you'll be able to withstand a lot of stuff. If there's nothing to draw on, then you'll feel emotionally bankrupt. And trust me, emotionally bankrupt people live in a state of constant fear.

I encourage each and every one of you who's been knocked down by betrayal to make your own journey. It's worth the work it takes, to reach nirvana – a far better place than you've ever known before – a place where you can love and live authentically!

- Rebecca Rosenblat

Chapter 27

New Beginnings, Happy Endings

John and Jane had booked a three-hour session with me – an hour for travel and two hours for the actual "session."

They'd requested that I come to their lake house nearby. I suspected that they had something extra special planned, so I cleared my entire afternoon – it was a Friday anyway.

When I pulled up into their driveway, I heard angelic harp music wafting from behind the house.

Their front door had a sign that requested that I go around the side and meet them at the dock.

The dock was covered with flowers tied to various posts, which led to a little canopy at the very end.

I was part of an elite crowd – John and Jane, their pastor, and the harpist.

John and Jane had decided to re-do their vows.

Jane felt their marriage was a farce. John didn't agree with that, but he wanted to give Jane a new anniversary to celebrate each year nonetheless; one that marked their new life together.

As for the rings: Jane had stopped wearing her wedding ring, because she'd felt it was a meaningless symbol – again, John had thought otherwise.

Regardless, he had their rings melted down together, and had new ones made out of the old gold. It had the serenity prayer engraved on the inside, to guide them – always!

John started with, "It was the worst day and the best day of my life – the day that Jane discovered that I'd betrayed her. The worst day because of the pain I caused her – a pain that'll forever live inside me. The best day, because it started the journey that made me the man I am today ... the man that Jane deserves!"

Jane started to cry – tears of joy, this time – and only mouthed her vows, because words wouldn't come out. It didn't matter, since John felt each and every word, as it touched that painful place inside him; giving him hope that it would be healed one day – forgiven, but never forgotten!

It was a true privilege to walk alongside John and Jane, through their joys and sorrows, to get to that glorious day.

***

I encourage each and every one of you who's been knocked down by betrayal to make your own journey. It's worth the work it takes, to reach nirvana – a far better place than you've ever known before – a place where you can love and live authentically!

Like a jet that uses up 70% of it's energy during takeoff and only 30% to float around in space and land, the hardest work is in the beginning – but don't let that discourage you, because the flight is worth it. Yes, it will be painful at times – but no pain, no gain, right? As long as you can hold each others hand, the pain will be bearable and bring you closer together. Just keep your eyes on the relationship, not either party. You will get there I promise, provided you're both fully committed to it!

And that's why I do what I do; despite having some depleting days. The reward at the end is worth each step. Bon Voyage!

RECAP

- Life is a beautiful journey, where you should look for detours, not stop at dead ends.

- If you journey together, you have a witness to your adventure; if you journey alone, you can get lost, and your stories will die with you.

- Recovery and healing from a betrayal is a lot of work; but nothing is more rewarding than that labour of love. You'll end up in a better place than where you began – but both parties have to show up for the ride!

- If you can focus on taking care of each other's feelings, even through your toughest conversations, you'll stay on track. Don't get sucked into the content tube where you feel you have something to prove.

APPENDIX

NEEDS INVENTORY

Each party is to complete this inventory and give it to their partner. Once the exchange has been made, set a time – at least three days away – to discuss what you've learned about each other. Sharing information doesn't oblige you to meet every single need – for those which are difficult to negotiate, try to come up with a way of dealing with them the best you can. You may need several conversations, but keep going until you both feel good about where you're headed! And since sharing will make you emotionally vulnerable, it's important that you do the exercise in a loving and helpful manner!

Facts About Your Partner

1.   What types of things does your partner say or do that make you feel loved?

2.   What types of things does your partner say or do that make you feel unloved?

3.   What initially attracted you to your partner?

4.   What is your favorite thing that your partner does during love making?

5.   Does your partner touch you enough?

6.   Does your partner compliment you enough?

7. How/when does your partner make you feel special?

8.   Do you have an interest in a sexual activity that you haven't told your partner about?

9.   What scares you the most (if anything) about your relationship?

10. What is your favorite thing about your relationship?

11. What makes you feel alive? How can your partner help you with that and maintaining your joy and individuality?

12. Think about your impression of when you first met. What has changed since then?

13. Is there anything you think your partner isn't 100% truthful about?

14. What is the most hurtful thing your partner has ever said or done to you?

15. What thing does your partner do that you love? When was the last time they did it?

16. What is your favorite thing about your partner's body? Their mind?

17. Name a behavior of your partner's that irritates you.

18. What sets your partner apart from other people.

19. How do you feel when you're apart?

20. What does your partner contribute to your life?

21. What attracted you to your partner? What do you think attracted them to you?

22. What are some thoughts you have when you see your partner talking to an attractive member of the opposite sex?

23. How can your partner show you their support?

24. Have you ever worried that your partner would be unfaithful to you?

25. Have you ever thought about being unfaithful to your partner?

26. When do you most admire your partner?

27. Are you confident in how your partner feels about you? What could they do to increase that?

28. Do you think you spend too much time together? Too little?

29. Is your relationship less exciting now compared to when you first met? In what way?

30. What is your biggest fear?

Going Deeper

1.   List 3 things you love about your partner.

2.   List 3 things which challenge you about your partner.

3.   List 3 things you wish for your relationship, that aren't yet a part of it.

4.   List 3 things that you wish were different about your relationship.

5.   List 3 things that your partner does which make you feel they have your back.

6.   List 3 things your partner does which make you feel unimportant/rejected.

7.   Do you feel that you matter to your partner?

8.   Do you feel that your partner will come when you need them and reach out for them?

9.   Do you feel like a priority to your partner? Are they a priority for you?

10.   Does your partner know your dreams? Do they support them? If so, how?

What I Need from A Partner

Complete the following sentences:

1.   It's important that my partner recognizes the following as important to me:

2.   It's important to me that my partner considers fulfilling my following needs:

3.   I find the following characteristics about my partner to be irritating:

4.   I carry unresolved resentment in the following areas:

What Love Means to Me

Complete the following sentences:

1.   When I think of love, I think of:

2.   I feel loved when:

3.   In a relationship, I have the following needs (list everything from togetherness, to time for yourself, to your expectations of the relationship and your partner, to how you see money, kids, home, & leisure playing out, and a general sense of your two, five and ten year plans):

My Ideal Two Year Plan:

My Ideal Five Year Plan :

My Ideal Ten Year Plan:

What Sex Means to Me

Complete the following sentences:

1.   I want intimacy to include:

2.   I feel desired when:

3.   Ideally, I'd like my sex life to include the following, for me to feel satisfied:

4.   Whether or not my partner takes care of their appearance ties into my desirability to them in the following ways:

Caring Exercise:

List all the ways your partner can show you caring (calling you through the day, putting away cell phone during dinner, kissing you when you come home, holding the door open for you, cooking for you, rubbing your feet, giving you a chance to decompress when you come home, surprising you with thoughtful gestures, making intimacy a priority, helping you with household chores, complimenting you more often, dressing up for you, etc.). There's sound evidence which suggests that when you start re-doing things you did in the initial stages of your relationship, or start doing things which are important to your partner, even though they may not be important to you, you end up creating closeness.

Other Comments: (List everything that's important to you that we may have missed – this is your chance to clarify those needs and irritations, from bad breath to partner letting themselves go, from not feeling like a priority to feeling ignored, from having sexual challenges to not liking how your partner tastes during oral sex, from being concerned about drinking and spending to laziness and depression, and so on, and so on. Don't leave anything out. Of course being honest is different from being brutally honest – this is not an opportunity to hurt each other! Be careful to maintain a 5 to 1 ratio for positive to negative comments.)

BIBLIOGRAPHY

Must Read Books, in order of appearance

1. Reinventing Your Life: The Breakthrough Program to End Negative Behavior ... and Feel Great Again, by Dr. Jeffrey Young & Janet Klosko

2. Intimacy Anorexia: The Hidden Addiction in Your Marriage, by Dr. Doug Weiss

3. Facing the Shadow: Starting Sexual and Relationship Recovery, by Dr. Patrick Carnes

4. The Five Languages of Apology: How to Experience Healing in All Your Relationships, by Dr. Gary Chapman & Jennifer Thomas

5. Codependent No More: How to Stop Controlling Others and Start Caring for Yourself, by Melody Beattie

6. Daring to Trust: Opening Ourselves to Real Love and Intimacy, by Dr. David Richo

7. The Five Love Languages: The Secret to Love that Lasts, by Dr. Gary Chapman

8. 5 Sex Languages, by Dr. Doug Weiss

9. Hold me Tight: Seven Conversations for a Lifetime of Love, by Dr. Sue Johnson

About the Author

Rebecca Rosenblat is a Registered Psychotherapist, Certified Sex Addiction Therapist, and Couple's Counselor, who specializes in trauma and betrayal work.

Rebecca has hosted five TV shows (more viewers than David Letterman's Late Show in her broadcast region), plus two radio shows. In total, she's given more than 1,000 hours of guidance to millions of people worldwide.

Beyond that, Rebecca has written seven published books: *An Eastern Seduction; Smooth as Silk; Broken Promises; How to Drive Your Lover Wild with Pleasure; Seducing your Man – the honeymoon was just the beginning; Sexual Power*; and now, *Overcoming Betrayal*.

Rebecca lives in Toronto with her family, where she runs her private practice, is an associate at a clinic, and teaches, transforming thousands of lives.

Her passion is to help people become the best they can be; and have the best relationships possible! To learn more about Rebecca, please visit the author's website: *www.TalkWithRebecca.com.*

To reach Rebecca, book an appointment, register for an intensive, or access free articles, video clips, and social media posts, visit: *www.RelationshipAndSexuality.com.*

"It's your life; make it exceptional!"
~ Rebecca

Overcoming Betrayal / Rebecca Rosenblat

Manor House
www.manor-house.ca